Taylor Caldwell's

ON GROWING UP TOUGH . . .

"A BLUNT AND PENETRATING COMPARISON OF HER OWN CHILDHOOD AND THAT OF THE REBELLIOUS YOUNGER GENERATION. . . . YOU MAY APPLAUD, YOU MAY CURSE, BUT YOU WON'T ESCAPE ONE NAGGING QUESTION: WHAT IF SHE'S RIGHT?"
—*San Diego Union*

"*ON GROWING UP TOUGH* SHOULD BE READ BY EVERY AMERICAN, YOUNG OR OLD, IN THE SAME SPIRIT IN WHICH IT IS WRITTEN: HUMOROUS, CRITICAL, OBJECTIVE BUT WITH A DEEP UNDERSTANDING OF HUMAN NATURE."
—*Fort Wayne Journal-Gazette*

"YOU'RE NOT LIKELY TO PUT THIS ONE DOWN UNTIL THE LAST LINE IS DEVOURED AND DIGESTED."
—*Charleston Sunday News & Courier*

" 'MUST' READING FOR THE WEAKLY LOAFERS AND CRY-BABIES WHO MOAN ABOUT AMERICA AND HOW TOUGH IT IS TO MAKE THE GRADE."
—*Union Leader*

D1222719

TAYLOR CALDWELL

ON GROWING UP TOUGH

A FAWCETT CREST BOOK

Fawcett Publications, Inc., Greenwich, Conn.

ON GROWING UP TOUGH

THIS BOOK CONTAINS THE COMPLETE TEXT OF THE ORIGINAL HARDCOVER EDITION.

A Fawcett Crest Book reprinted by arrangement with The Devin-Adair Company.

Library of Congress Catalog Card Number: 77-156276

Selection of the Anti-Communist Book Club, October 1972
Selection of the Veritas Book Club, October 1972

Acknowledgments: Most of the material in this book has previously appeared in *American Opinion;* other parts were first published in *National Review* and the *Buffalo Courier Express.* Grateful acknowledgment is hereby given to all three.

Printed in the United States of America
March 1973

Dedicated

to

ANNE McILHENNEY MATTHEWS

Contents

1. MRS. BUTTONS   9
2. IRMA JONES NEVER CAME BACK   17
3. THE DAY I WAS ABSOLUTELY PERFECT   30
4. SHARING   44
5. THE PURPLE LODGE   51
6. THE CHILD-LOVERS   57
7. LEARNING THE LIBERAL LINGO   65
8. ONOMATOPOEIA   73
9. PIONEERING IN KENTUCKY   79
10. WHAT HAPPENED TO AMERICAN MEN?   96
11. WOMEN'S LIB   103
12. T.L.C.—KEEP YOUR PAWS OFF ME!   118
13. LUV AND THE LAW   122
14. DOLTS AND LOVE CULTISTS   126
15. PLASTIC PEOPLE   132
16. WHY NOT A SPUVV?   138
17. ON HIPPIES   148

1

Mrs. Buttons

I began being a conservative when I was very young. A Liberal aunt of mine, who had never herself been in need of anything material, had a deep passion for the Poor, from whom she was very careful to keep far, far away. While we still lived in England, where I was born, Auntie would frequently gather together outworn garments which her family had discarded and prepare them for the Women's Guild of our local Anglican Church. She would sit before the fireplace, I recall, and singing some sad Scots or Irish ballad in a very moving soprano, she would carefully snip every single button off the clothing.

I was very young indeed when this practice of Auntie's suddenly seemed outrageous to me. "Auntie," I demanded, "what will the poor do for buttons?"

Auntie had remarkable hazel eyes, and they usually glittered on me unpleasantly. They did so now. "They can buy them," she snapped. "They're only a tuppence a card."

I pondered. If people were so poor that they had to wear other people's cast-offs, then they certainly were too poor to buy buttons. I pointed this out to Auntie. She smacked me fiercely for my trouble and then began:

"A wicked, wicked girl!" screamed Auntie. "She has no heart for the poor!"

My uncle, hearing Auntie's shrill cries, stormed out of his studio and demanded, "Now, what in hell's the matter?"

Auntie pointed a shaking, furious finger at me. "Your niece," she said, "doesn't want me to give these clothes—these poor old worthless rags—to the poor!"

I was standing up now having recovered from Auntie's blow. "If they're rags," I said, reasonably, "why should the poor want them, anyway? And she's taken off all the buttons."

"Impudence," bellowed Uncle, who like Auntie was a flaming Liberal and also very fond of making a great show of loving the Poor (whom he had never met). And he grabbed me and thrashed me on the spot. I am afraid I didn't ardently love those relatives after that, which was sinful, of course. But from that day on, buttons had a special significance for me. One rich relative did answer my cynical question about the button snipping with the brief reply, "It's thrifty, and I suppose, Janet, that's something you'll never be." Thrift is an estimable virtue, but somehow when I encounter thrifty Liberals—and they are inevitably tight with their own money—I always seem to see those damned buttons being snipped off the clothing for the poor. I often think of the old couplet written by some Englishman who ought to be immortalized:

> *To spread the wealth the Communist's willing:*
> *He'll tax your pennies and keep his shilling.*

To this day I often find myself referring to male and female Liberals as "Mr. Buttons" or "Mrs. Buttons," among the less invidious names I employ when I am in form.

My Grandmother—never Granny—was not a Liberal. She was a short red-haired, belligerent, and very gay little Irishwoman who, when necessary, was tight with a quid but could be lavish at times and would slip a small girl a sovereign on her birthday with the wise admonishment, "And ye'll not be telling your Dad or Mum, if ye're sensible." I was always sensible on those occasions. Grandmother had a low opinion of her offspring, all four of them, and their wives. If she had a favorite, it was I, who was named after her. I loved her conversation, and she would always listen to me, so one day when I was visiting her in Leeds I told her about those accursed buttons.

"Niver trust anyone who weeps for the poor," said Grandmother, "unless they're damned poor, themselves." I've found that a sound rule-of-thumb to this very day. This does not mean I am against the poor, and never help them. I do. But I first make sure they want to help themselves. And I don't weep over them.

When I was four years old and just about to embark on my studies at Miss Brothers' "exclusive school for young ladies and gentlemen" in Manchester, my parents decided to brief me on the matter. I already had a furious dislike for the school, which I had never seen, and was upstairs in my bedroom brooding about it, while the cold September rains of England lashed the windowpanes. I received the summons from my elderly parents—respectively twenty-two and twenty-six at that time—to join them before the parlor fire downstairs. I rapidly ran over my day's sins in my mind while I reluctantly went downstairs to receive what undoubtedly would be a deserved punishment. I decided the major sin was being in the jampots that afternoon, in the scullery, while Mama was resting. So I was understandably apprehensive when I entered the parlor, and my parents' expressions did nothing to relieve my fears.

"Stand there, on the hearth," said Papa, fixing me with his cold blue eyes. Mama's stare was no less forbidding. So. I stood on the hearth, trembling. My thrashings were never taken meekly, but with some telling kicks on my part, for though I was only four I was very big and strong.

"You are going to school tomorrow," said Papa, as if I didn't know the disastrous day. "I will take you when I go to my studio at the *Manchester Guardian,* at eight o'clock. And I want to warn you," Papa added in a terrible voice of doom and threat, "if you do not behave in Miss Brothers' School, and if I hear from her one word of your mischief or insolence, you will be thoroughly thrashed. Is that clear?"

"Yes, Papa," I replied.

"You will be neat and tidy, eat nicely, be polite and obedient at all times, and never answer back," said Mama with severity, "You will learn. Your father will inspect your lessons every night. Is that understood?"

"Yes, Mama," I replied.

"And you'll never be tardy," said Papa, who hated to get up in the morning and hated to be on time and had to be rousted out of bed and hurried by Mama every day. But at least he thought promptness was a virtue, if a foul nuisance, and never permitted a child to comment on inconsistencies.

I could see that my parents were considering the sound principle of "never a lick amiss," so I hastily curtseyed and got out of there up to my bedroom, where I spent most of my time. I busied myself laying out my woolen frock for the morrow. I then polished my boots. After that I took my bath, cleaned my teeth, brushed my long red hair, went to bed and contemplated how much I could cut out of my elaborate prayers. I decided not to speak to the Archangel Michael that night, nor to all the saints,

and to omit Miss Brothers—whom I had never met—
from my petitions. But I did pray for dear Mama and
Papa, and for two dolls at Christmas, and went to sleep.
Without the resentments, either, that the child psychologists say children always feel when they are sure they are
being treated unjustly. It never occurred to me that there
was any injustice in my life. I lived the life of the usual
middle-class British child, and all my playmates were
treated firmly and thumped regularly by their parents.
C'est la vie. Children are tough little animals, not tender
blossoms.

The next day was vile, as only English autumns can be
vile, with heavy gray rain and shouting winds. Papa refused to be stirred from bed, even by doughty Mama,
until nine, and it was now half-past six. "Let her go, herself," he said. "She knows the way."

I did. Mama's maid-of-all-work boiled me a hard egg,
which I loathed, and made me some burned bacon and
toast and a kipper and some lukewarm tea, and I got into
my mackintosh over a warm coat, pulled on my tam-o'-
shanter, and went out into the wild cold weather—for a
walk of well over a mile. I was about half a minute late,
for which I was coldly rebuked and warned never to repeat, then introduced to my red-cheeked mates, all as
abominably healthy as I and all studiously bent over slates
and books at their tables.

It was a long and arduous and punishing day, and did
not end until four o'clock. We worked on the alphabet,
and at writing figures up to ten. No "reading readiness,"
you will observe, or playtimes, or kindergarten, or fingerpainting, or songs—except for "God Save the King" and
a couple of hymns—and there was a special prayer for our
dear guides and mentors, the King, the Parliament, the
Empire, our parents and our teachers. The Union Jack
was gravely saluted, and at four o'clock we genuflected
to the Crucifix on the wall, as we had genuflected before
and after luncheon and tea. Then we were dismissed, to

worse weather, our hands and feet icy, for Miss Brothers did not believe in fires until October. But we exuberantly raced home, our faces wet with rain and our boots splashing in puddles, and our Daily Report in our pockets. We weren't tired at all, after eight hours.

That night, after high tea, I was introduced—as a grownup person now—to laying fires in the parlor, the dining room, and my parents' room. This had been the usual job for Agnes, the maid, but as I was now a schoolgirl it was my job. I thought nothing of it, nor was disturbed that I was called down from my bedroom at nine to wipe my parents' dinner dishes—a new job. The scullery was warm, and Agnes had many blood-curdling tales of beasties and ghoulies to amuse me.

I wasn't spanked at school or by my parents for a whole week, and very soon I was reading and writing simple sentences, and was being introduced to Latin. There was little playtime in my busy life from then on, only half an hour's recreation at school, after lunch, and what I could snatch at home between high tea and my parents' dishes and the laying of new fires for the next day. Sunday was no quiet day. I spent three hours in Sunday-school, and helped Agnes with the dinner dishes, then was given an Improving Book—Bible stories—as a fun-time project, until it was time for bed. Incidentally, children of that time and place were not permitted to waste the precious hours in bed. Bed time was between nine and ten, and you were out of the quilts before six.

I was never sick under this rigorous treatment. By the time I was seven I had had two years of Latin and one of French, and was reading Shakespeare's Sonnets, not to mention minor poets, and had had a good grounding in history and geography. No guidance counselors, no twitterings on the part of teachers, no worry for parents, no soft patting hands, no cherishing. We were being prepared for Life.

Was I "cowed"? Not a bit of it! Was I "fearful, insecure, timid"? Don't be silly. I knew that life was for real, and it was up to me to deserve living, or God help me. No one else would. I was constantly being taught to be grateful to my parents for condescending to give me life, and to my teachers for teaching me, and to God for letting me live. Above all, I was taught to have an independent and searching mind, to scorn weak tears, to detest dependency on the part of anybody, to be brave and to endure. To sin was intolerable. To defend oneself was demanded at all times.

When I was five I had a baby brother, and I had to help with his care. I rocked him in his cradle—the only time British children were indulged. I prepared his bed, helped to feed him, folded his diapers, and sat in his room until he was asleep, for fear he would smother under all those eiderdowns. I wheeled him in his carriage after school, and on Saturdays and Sundays, between times. I amused him. It was all part of the job of living. A year later, incredible as it may seem, I also won the National Gold Medal for my essay on Charles Dickens.

One day my father said to me, "We are going to America, and I hear it is a very foolish and uncultured country, and so I am warning you beforehand. No nonsense, when you go to school there! They indulge their children. You are not going to be indulged. You will keep yourself to yourself, as at home. And another thing: Every tub must stand on its own bottom. You are six years old and not a child any longer, and we have a younger child, and so you must be self-reliant—or else."

I was, too. And still am. My parents, as much as they could, carried on the Spartan life for me, and now for my brother, in spite of the softness in America for children. I was earning my spending-money when I was seven after I finished my school work and my chores at home. Saturday and Sunday were tough days . . . ironing, mending, darning, snow-shoveling, grass-cutting, glass polishing, and sundry other arduous tasks, and homework and Sunday-school, and church twice a day. I was lucky to get eight hours of sleep. And I got the Jesse Ketchum Medal and won prizes at school and in state competitions, for essays and short stories. Of course, I could never master mathematics, but as my parents were weak on the subject, too, I was indulged in that one, but that one only.

When I was ten I was working at the local market on Saturday filling up bags and helping wait on customers. I looked all of fifteen. When I was indeed fifteen I held a full-time job as a secretary. (I had paid for my own tuition at the Hurst Business School.) After work I went to night high school. Sunday was my "free" day. I had a Sunday-school class of my own, then hurried home to help with dinner, prepare my clothing for the next day, and do my homework. I was up at half-past five to get my father's breakfast and mine and my brother's, wash up, hastily glance over schoolwork, and was out in the street at six-forty on the way to work. Not much time for loitering!

In America of those days there was no time to be a "teenager," or to have the adolescent "turmoils." None of my schoolmates ended up on welfare rolls, even during the Great Depression, nor were any of them criminals, thieves, murderers, or whiners. Our parents, even in America before the Depression—had been tough, perhaps most not as tough as mine, but all happily tough enough.

2

Irma Jones Never Came Back

When I am asked, "Why are you a hater of Liberalism?" I invariably reply, "I have had painful, scarring, personal experiences with it and it is not just an ideological matter. As a peaceful person, I am willing to live and let live. But the Liberal will not, if he can help it, let you live in peace, or, coming down to the matter, let you live at all."

I have had scores of agonizing encounters with Liberals, but in my memory the worst occurred when I was eleven years old, and just about as happy as a child that age can be. (Children are not really "happy," as their teachers and parents would like to believe. Coming in increasing contact with reality, as the days pass, children suffer unavoidable agonies which they cannot communicate.)

The children in my class at school were reasonably clean, obedient, and studious, which is all anyone can ask of a child in the throes of growing up and learning about life. I had several friends, notably Irma Jones, who was the envy of all us girls. Her widowed mother was a dressmaker, and Irma had dazzling clothes and preened in them. But she was a kind girl at heart and would invite a select few of us home after school to partake of her mother's delightful little cakes and homemade candies, such as we did not get at home, our mothers believing that anything sugary was bound to ruin our teeth. Irma had beautiful teeth, so here went another illusion about our mothers' omniscience.

Fanny and Anna were twin girls, very pretty with fair, curling hair and big blue eyes. The fact that they were almost abnormally bright did not make the rest of us hate them, because they were pleasant little girls and could throw a mean baseball on the playground and would democratically share any goodies in their lunchbaskets with the rest of us who had more sketchy mothers.

I should say, then, that Irma Jones and Fanny and Anna were about the three most popular girls in our class.

It is a canon law of childhood that you must be suspicious of your new teacher in September and be prepared to dislike her. She is on trial for a month at least. After that a modus vivendi sets in, and later, if the teacher happens to be half-way decent, mutual regard is established. But I was mistrustful of Miss Blank from the start. She had such a staring and watery eye, and would gulp soulfully, and gaze at us with Love. I knew there was something wrong with her. I confided this to my dear friends, Irma Jones and Fanny and Anna, and a few others who would listen. "You'll get over it," they told me. But I knew I should not. I had a female relative with the same sort of tremulous voice as Miss Blank, and the same pinched and intense expression and the same look of Love, and she was generally known in the family as The Bitch. However, I had other things on my mind so I began to endure Miss Blank. (I had just been appointed head of the Arkansas Street Regulars, a baseball club.)

Previous teachers had begun the day with the Pledge of Allegiance to the Flag, the Lord's Prayer, and a simple

hymn. No Protestant, Catholic, or Jewish parent had ever
objected to any of this. Miss Blank, however, to the bored
relief of a lot of us little unregenerates, dispensed with all
but the Pledge of Allegiance, which she hurried through
with an air of annoyance. She then briskly referred us to
our books, which we felt was unfair. The unused fifteen
minutes should have been occupied with more pleasant
things. We were cheated, and now I know we were cheated
in more ways than one.

Then, two days before Thanksgiving, I learned what a
Liberal was, and I have never recovered from the wound.

Portentously, at precisely two o'clock of an ennui-ridden
afternoon, Miss Blank closed her book, clasped her hands
on it and surveyed us with her wide eyes. She gulped sol-
emnly, turning her face from one to the other of us. We
became fascinated. Maybe someone had died, we thought.
The more optimistic of us began to hope that we'd be
told that school was out until next Monday. The air in
the chalky room became charged with interest. There was
a scandal going around among the teachers, and we
children, right down to the first grade, knew all the details. Perhaps, I thought, Miss Blank was about to fill in
some gaps, though I doubted that; we knew what filled
the gaps.

Miss Blank cleared her throat. "Children I want to give
you a lesson today in Tolerance and Love."

The faintest groan came from the sturdier boys; this
was bound to be dull. They had never heard of Tolerance,
but Miss Blank was an uninspired teacher and she would
have nothing interesting to say about anything.

Miss Blank's suffused eye slowly settled on Irma Jones.
Irma wore a bright blue velvet dress with real lace at the
neck and wrists. "Dear Irma," sang Miss Blank. Then she
engaged the rest. "You must not despise Irma because—
she—is—a—Negress," said Miss Blank. "She cannot help
it. You must not look at her color. She is just as human
as the rest of you."

All heads swung to Irma, who suddenly cowered in her seat. So help me, until that evil moment, none of us had ever noticed that Irma was colored! She was just a kid like the rest of us, with nicer clothes and a more indulgent mother and somewhat better manners. Now we stared at Irma, hypnotized. She was different from us! She was apart from us. The children about Irma began to move away from her in their seats, with uncomfortable faces and averted eyes. I could feel that something intensely wicked had flowed from Miss Blank's area, and without a formed reason, then, I began to hate her.

Miss Blank's gulp was loud and righteous in the silent room. She then swung those abominable eyes upon Fanny and Anna, who looked back at her confusedly. "Nor," sang Miss Blank, "must you hate Fanny and Anna because they are Jews. You must love them dearly, as your Fellow Men, in spite of what you are taught in your Sunday-schools."

No one had ever taught us to despise Jews in our churches. We had heard, with the vagueness of childhood, that Our Lord had been born in some far-off and only half-believed-in country called Israel, among His fellow countrymen who were called Jews, and that some of His countrymen had loved Him to the death and others had hated Him. (It was part of the incomprehensible way of grown-ups, we had decided, and not to be taken too seriously.) But now, all at once, poor pretty Fanny and Anna had become those who had hated Our Lord. They were responsible for His crucifixion! What had once been only a part of Christianity now became the crucial, the damning, the hateful part. The Crucifixion was now not only God's plan for the salvation of man and the sign of His eternal love for us, but an act of infamy of which little Fanny and Anna were the main criminals. From some bulky boy in the background came awful words, "Christ-killers!"

The shrinking from Irma was nothing compared now

with the shrinking from Fanny and Anna. But I could only look at Miss Blank. I felt an adult desire to go to her desk and beat her into the floor. My young heart burned as no child's heart should be made to burn. I am sure I was not alone.

The silence in the room was the silence that fills an execution chamber. Then, while almost all eyes glared at Irma and Fanny and Anna, Irma rose with the immense dignity of her people and, head held high, walked slowly and firmly to the door. She closed it behind her. While we still sat frozen in our horror of everything, Fanny and Anna rose also, their faces white and trembling with tears, and left also. Miss Blank waited until the door was shut then she fixed us with her accusing eyes.

"You see," she thundered, "what you have done to Those Poor Children! You are very bad indeed."

We said nothing. We thought the monster had done with it. But now it was my turn. Her eyes fixed themselves on me. "And there's Janet Caldwell," she said, and at once the new hating gaze of my fellows moved in my direction. "In spite of the American Revolution, you must not hate Janet because she was born in England!"

Now those were the days, just prior to the first World War, when the British were not loved in America, nor were they to be loved until 1917, with some remaining reservations. I had accepted that fact. But I had sung the national anthem as loud as anyone; I had as fervently pledged allegiance to the flag. I had not considered myself different from my native-born American schoolmates. It is true that at home my parents had had some derisive things to say about American customs, but I ignored them as all children ignore the words of adults—most of the time. My father had told me that one of my ancestors had fought with, not against, George Washington, before he had returned to Scotland to found his family. But that had not been important, either. The Arkansas Street Regulars were the most important thing in my life; we

were trying to get a catcher's mitt and a new baseball
bat, without much success.

I sat transfixed by the newly despising eyes of my
friends. Then the bulky boy in the rear said, "Redcoat!"
I had had it.

I am usually a peaceful person, slow to wrath. But
what I had witnessed concerning Irma Jones and Fanny
and Anna, and what I was suffering now, filled me with
the blackest rage. I stood up and hurled a book at Miss
Blank. It caught her smartly on the cheek and she howled
and fell sideways. Then I went to the door, followed
by whistles and jeers and exclamations of dismay.

I stood in the hallway and the blackness in my heart
rose to my eyes and I could hear my heart pounding. I
hoped I had killed Miss Blank. Then I went down to see
our principal whom I knew as a good man, and kind and
sensible. I told him what had happened. He listened
gravely. He said not a thing; he only shook his head. After
a while he told me I could go home.

Of course, in the way of children, I did not tell my
parents. Mama was a fiery little woman. She would go
at once, I knew, to Miss Blank and tell her a thing or
two before her students, and that would make matters
worse. I had come a long way in knowledge. I developed
a sick headache that night, my first, and so stayed at
home until Monday. And when I returned Miss Blank
was no longer there; we had a new teacher.

But Irma Jones never came back, either, and neither did
Fanny and Anna. They had transferred to another school.
However, I was stuck. I was the "foreigner," and shunned.
I was removed as president of the Arkansas Street Regulars. I never got over it. I never shall.

Many years later, my husband and I had a piece of
property to sell. One hot summer day a white man arrived
in a car with his colored chauffeur. Our housekeeper was
a colored woman, a member of our family whose law
was not to be challenged when it came to children and

the affairs of the household. The white man, complaining of the heat, sat down with our housekeeper and drank lemonade with her. The chauffeur, a much younger man, wanted me to show him the grounds. It was evident that he considered his employer not one with good judgment, so it was up to him to decide. I took the chauffeur around the grounds, employing my salesmanship, and he remained courteously unimpressed, like all potential buyers.

Apparently the property did not come up to the standards of the chauffeur, for we never saw either of them again.

But I saw my neighbors. The next day a delegation of ladies, red-faced, and in a temper, arrived to see me. They refused refreshments, so I fixed myself some bourbon and ice and wondered about the infestation. I was soon enlightened. The leader of the ladies drew a deep breath and then burst out, "We understand that you are going to sell this property to *niggers!*"

I winced at the ugly word, "What?" I asked. "What are 'niggers?' "

She flounced and glared at me. "You know very well what I mean! We saw you showing them around."

Again, I wish to affirm I am a peaceable person. But suddenly I saw little Irma Jones' face. I stood up. "Get out of here," I said. "If you don't go at once I'll call the police."

I did not see the leader of the ladies again until about two years ago. She appeared at our house with a petition for me to sign "against segregation in the South, and for strict adherence to the Supreme Court's 'law'."

I asked the lady to sit down. I knew her reputation by now. She was a great Liberal. There was not a Cause that she was not dabbling in. She was against prayer in schools—"a separation of Church, and State, you know." She was against all kinds of "bias." She clamored for better housing conditions for the colored people in the city, and the wretchedly cold and newly arriving Puerto Ricans. She

was all for free speech, if it concerned the free speech of
her fellow Liberals. She belonged to this league, and she
belonged to that.

"In the first place," I said to her, flexing my muscles
with anticipatory enjoyment, "you have forgotten a basic
part of the Constitution. The U.S. Supreme Court does not
pass 'laws.' It only interprets the Constitution. In the
second place, my observation has shown me that since
that Court voted that *decision* every one in the country
has become color-conscious. This is cruel, and dangerous.
The Court has divided the white man from his neighbor.
Was that the real intention, anyway? Is that what you
like about it?"

Her florid face became bright crimson. She shook a
gloved finger at me. "It is evident," she said in a menacing voice, "that you don't like Negroes, that you are a
reactionary."

"I don't know if I like Negroes or not," I said. "I've
never met any, not having been to Africa. If you are
referring to colored people, then I know dozens, and I
know their bitter anxiety these days, and their justified
alarm. Moreover, it seems to me that you visited me not
too long ago to accuse me of trying to sell some property
to what you referred to as 'niggers.' I think the newspapers would like to know about that. Now, will you kindly
get the hell out of my house?"

She jumped up very fast, and that was quite an accomplishment, considering her obesity. She could have
murdered me on the spot, and I hoped she would try. My
father taught me boxing and wrestling when I was a child
and I wanted to take the lady on.

"There's a *difference*," she spluttered, "to being just
to them and having them live next door to you!" Then she
rushed out with a frightened, backward look.

Yes, I could have told her there *is* a "difference." You
despise your colored neighbor in your cold, hypocritical
heart. But it is not the style, these days, to be frank, to be

candid about aversions "on the basis of creed or color."
And you are all for style, for modishness, for "progress."
You want to force the colored man to live next door or
in the next apartment to the white man whether he wants
to or not, and most of the time he'd prefer not to. You
fawn on the colored man at public gatherings, until he is
embarrassed half to death. I have news for you! You are
more than he can endure; you are making his life intolerable. He no longer thinks of himself as an American. He
thinks of himself as a Negro, someone apart from his
fellowman, something alien, something strange, something
to be "tolerated."

How dare you force that ignominy on a fellow creature,
who is the same soul in the eyes of God as you are? (But
I forgot; you don't believe in God.)

How dare you call to the attention of a white man that
his colored fellowman is to be "loved" and not to be
treated merely as a co-worker or a friend, or even as an
enemy if the two are incompatible? Before God, you have
done the most evil of all things: You have set man against
his brother, white man against black, black against white.

Is that your intention? I think it is. You have your
reasons, and I know them. You want to destroy our free
country. A house divided against itself cannot stand.

My father was a Republican. Mama was a Democrat.
I doubt if either of them voted regularly, or at all, in the
manner of most Americans, foreign-born or not. Election
times were spirited. There were bonfires on the streets,
and Papa and I would go out and enjoy them. He'd have
a bonfire, too, no matter who won the elections. For, you
see, free elections were the celebrations of a free people.
They are no longer. Now they are vicious battlegrounds,
and Republicans hate Democrats, and vice versa.

Up to 1933, when I was a very young woman, I never
knew if my friend or neighbor or co-worker was a Republican or a Democrat, and I could not have cared less.
Sometimes I voted for a Republican—I was a registered

one. But most of the time I split my ticket. I voted for
the great Al Smith, and nothing will shake my conviction
to this day that had we elected Mr. Smith there would
not have been a second World War. Hitler would have
vanished from interest-malnutrition. Stalin might have remained and died almost unknown behind his grim mountains. There might even have been no advance of
Communism in the world, no present terror. And, no wars.
For Mr. Smith would have been reelected again in 1932.

You cheered for your candidate in those innocent days,
and whether or not he was elected you built bonfires and
celebrated. You did not know if your close associates were
Democrats or Republicans. You never heard the word
liberal. In fact, Republicans in those days were considered
more "advanced" than the average Democrat, even in
the North. They were also bigger spenders in public office,
believe it or not. In fact, FDR expressed himself as horrified that we had a *twenty billion* dollar public debt in
1932 and he had a right to be horrified.

I dimly remember that when I was a very young child
Teddy Roosevelt was considered "progressive." I better
remember that you could buy a huge stick of gum then,
in honor of Teddy's Big Stick. But Teddy's progressive-
ness appears downright medieval in comparison with what
is going on these days among "modern" Republicans and
"liberal" Democrats.

The Liberal did not really make his appearance until
1933 in any significant way in America. Though it may
surprise some Republicans, Mr. Roosevelt said in 1933,
"The liberal is a man both of whose feet are firmly
planted in the air." Mr. Roosevelt was too kind to him.
We've all been too kind. It's time we stopped being dan-
gerously ignorant fools, whether we are Republicans or
Democrats. For the Liberal is the enemy of us both.

From 1932 on, the Liberal seized control of the public
means of communication, with rare exceptions. How he

managed this so smoothly I don't know. He must have been lying under the surface of our national life.

The Liberal is all for a free press—meaning free for his masters. But it is not free for all Americans. Many are the writers, once famous thirty years ago, who are not read today or even known, though I remember them. They refused to become part of the conspiracy against America, refused to shout for a second World War, refused to follow the Liberal/Communist line. So, they quietly disappeared from the awareness of readers. But those writers who obeyed the Liberal are still doing excellently today. They get Nobel prizes; the press constantly mentions them; the columnists relate little anecdotes about them. Clubs invite them to speak. Universities adore them and call them "serious" writers. (If you are an anti-Communist you are, per se, *not* a serious writer. I know. I've been through this.)

A writer, like an actor, needs publicity. If he is ignored, then he is not read, even by those who are in agreement with him. He gets no free advertising. When John Dos Passos was following the Liberal line the press adored him. He had book selections galore. His name was read everywhere. When he awoke from the nightmare the press suddenly became silent about him. This is what the Liberal means by "tolerance." He will endure no opinion that differs from his own.

The American people, no matter their political party, are basically conservative and love their country. The Liberal knows this better than anyone else. So he fills his press and all the other public means of communication with Liberal lies and treacheries so that the average conservative American begins uneasily to wonder if there is something wrong with him, if he is out of step with his fellow-Americans. So, against all his convictions, he begins to mouth the Liberal Line. He must be in style. Man is a herd animal! He doesn't want to be shunned or outcast. He doesn't want to think he is "intolerant." He does not realize it is his enemy who is intolerant and vicious and is deftly manipulating him.

Newspapermen, even those who work for ostensibly "conservative" newspapers have told me confidentially that they can never get a byline unless they write something liberal. The Liberal is everywhere, they tell me. His intolerant blue pencil is forever busy, he slants news. Look at our magazines. Let any reader tell me of a single magazine which numbers its circulation in the millions that is truly conservative. Occasionally, to show how "tolerant" he is, the inner Liberal will permit a conservative article in his magazine. But the editorial in the same issue will be overwhelmingly liberal. Show me the conservative writer—no matter how well known—and there are still a few of us—who are given bids by large magazines for articles. Very, very few.

I know many movie-makers who are basically conservative and good men. But they have to go to the banks for their money. And, invariably, there is a powerful Liberal in the bank who wants to see the script. Let that script be anti-Communist or truly patriotic or honestly revealing about the heart of America, and the movie-maker will not get money to produce his picture. Movie-makers have told me so.

Let an innocent schoolteacher—who believes that the Liberal is "tolerant"—try to inspire patriotism and all the great virtues of our Republic in her students, and she will soon hear from Liberals on the schoolboard. The girls have told me all about it, weeping. The Liberal, who is so very "tolerant," insists that she speak of One World, that she subtly ridicule patriotism, that she spread the canard that the American Revolution was "really against the working man." She must imply that our Constitution is an out-grown instrument; she must twist and deform it to please her liberal masters on the schoolboard. If she will not, then she is constantly transferred until she is exhausted, or resigns, or, if she is still on probation her contract is not renewed. She is a "disrupting" force in the schoolroom. She is not "tolerant."

You cannot argue with a Liberal. Meet him in someone's living-room and he will soon probe to discover "what you are." If you are not of his brand, then he is after you. He can be insulting, will not endure your opinions. He shouts that you are "intolerant." At the worst, he will insinuate that because you do not have his own mind you are an anti-Semite or you are anti-Negro. If he is politically powerful, he will try to destroy you. I speak from experience.

3

The Day I Was Absolutely Perfect

The Easter Sunday when I was seven years old was extraordinarily luminous, warm, mild, sweet—a rare thing in upper New York State. That, combined with the fact that the contents of my Easter basket were unusually delicious, put me in an exalted mood. I sat on the porch steps in the early twilight, while my father and mother, ages twenty-nine and twenty-six, respectively, still dozed after the mountainous dinner Mama had served three hours before. My little brother, two years old, to whom I had given a nasty nickname, was also drowsing. The street basked in blue and green shadows. It was so very still. And holy.

I munched a particularly luscious chocolate chicken, contemplated the meaning of the day, and burst into lovely tears. Then I came to a momentous decision. Emulating the saints, the servants of God, I would also be a saint. Later, much later, when I died, I would stand in the golden streets and cry "Hosannah!" with all the rest of the saints, and I would still be so young that Our Lord would pause near me, tenderly. I wept, ate a few jelly beans, then walked down the street with purpose.

Old Father Walsh was studying the early tulips and daffodils in his garden when I came upon him. I leaned against his greening hedge. I said, "I am going to be a saint, beginning tomorrow."

The good priest surveyed me with some well-justified mistrust, for though I had lived in this neighborhood only a year I was already celebrated. "Are you, Janet?" he asked uneasily. He paused. "Don't try too hard, dear," he added with wisdom.

I regarded him coldly. This was certainly no way to greet one who was on the path to sainthood. Father Walsh said, "I mean, it isn't too easy. Just do your best—" But I was already leaving this insensitive old man who didn't recognize a saint when he saw one in full new blossom. I returned home to find my aged mother yawning in the kitchen while she prepared tea. Papa sat nearby reading the Sunday newspaper. "I," I said to them, "am going to be a saint. Beginning tomorrow."

"Begin now," said Mama, the cynic, handing me a tea-towel.

The Day I Was Absolutely Perfect arrived in due course —the next day. I said my prayers with particular devotion, rose from my knees like a spring, and dressed with neatness. When I appeared in the kitchen Mama fell into an exaggerated display of astonishment, quite out of proportion I thought. "What! Are you actually washed and dressed and combed? Is it possible I don't have to drive you to it today?"

"Is the girl sick?" asked Papa, looking up from his Scottish oatmeal and boiled milk and treacle.

"I told you," I explained patiently. "I am going to be a saint, beginning today."

"She is sick," said Papa, with a worried look as he thought of doctors' bills.

Mama inspected me narrowly and with her familiar skepticism. "No," she decided at last, "she's in one of her moods. Just ignore her."

But it was impossible to ignore me. That's what is wrong with saints, I've discovered. You can never ignore them, whether you want to or not, especially when social workers, puritan busybees, psychiatrically-oriented school teachers, child psychologists, community directors, censors, and other dreary people come in their guise.

I proceeded, with an iron will and an iron chin, on my self-ordained path to holiness. I may have been wanting in many other virtues, but I certainly had never been accused of approaching things in a languid manner or with half-heartedness. The Polar Star has nothing, even now, on steadfastness when it comes to my resolute decisions. I began to make life miserable for everyone in my limited world, in the manner of other unfortunates who have rashly made up their minds to be do-gooders, come hell or high water. There's a lot to be said in sympathy for those who used to come in contact with the reformers of the past, and who displayed some human irritation in consequence, which resulted in unpleasant inventions like stakes and ropes and thumb-screws.

I loathed oatmeal. Mama could never cook it without burning it. She waited for one of my customary acid comments, her hand already poised. But I ate it meekly. This made Mama suspicious. She bent over and sniffed at my plate. The oatmeal was burned all right. "Can't you taste it?" she asked me, her black eyes sharp. "Yes, Mama," I said, softly. "I don't have a cold. I can taste it."

My little brother toddled into the kitchen, and, whining, up to the table. It was my automatic custom to slap him when he came near. I gave him a sweet and holy smile which so startled him that he howled. "What did you do to him?" cried Mama, whirling from the stove. Papa remarked with some disquiet, "The girl didn't do anything.

She didn't even scowl at the bairn. Perhaps he's sick, too."

Brother was Mama's darling, and she swung him up, wet pants and all, into her arms and soberly examined his contemptibly rosy face. Brother screamed in fright, burbling and pointing over Mama's shoulder at me. I gave him another of my new, sweet smiles and he buried his head in Mama's neck and shuddered. Papa fled to his studio and slammed the door after him. It took some time for Mama to calm little Brother. During this period I returned to my room and made my bed without being hounded to the task, dusted the furniture, said a few prayers gently, and hummed a hymn. The exaltation returned to me, and I went back to the kitchen without trying to sneak out with my skates as usual. "Mama dear," I said, "I've taken care of my room and now I'll do the dishes, all by myself, and scour the sink."

Mama reflected darkly. She fed Brother his breakfast. Then she said, "You're up to something."

With silent and tender resignation I did my tasks. Mama took Brother outside, rolling his go-cart with a hurried briskness. I watched them go, then for extra measure I scrubbed the kitchen floor, made my parents' bed, dusted some more, then went to church to refresh the inner saint. I looked at the beautiful statues, and smiled deeply, I prayed with much devotion. I could feel beams of light emanating from me. In this ominous state I emerged into the spring sunshine. And paused. There was nothing to do, now that I had become a saint. There wasn't even the accursed school to go to, where I could practice diligently. There was just nothing to do. So Satan licked his chops.

Usually, I would now be flying on my skates to the enchanting towpath to watch the barges go by and listen with delight to the swearing of the women on the houseboats and the cursing of the men, and play with the squatters' children. All this was forbidden by my parents, and always I had disobeyed. But in my new capacity as saint

I could not do this. I put on my skates, and thought of good deeds. I was a sturdy girl and turned a frequent keen penny by washing neighbors' windows, mowing their grass, going to the shops for them, churning ice cream, and doing sundry other tasks which their own offspring got out of one way or another. I didn't like to do these things but my allowance was five cents a week, and there was a candy and soda store on the corner which was very alluring.

I had a sudden inspiration. Putting on my radiant smile again I skated to the house of one of my clients, who was glad to see me. (Her own fat brats were having a fine time climbing the telephone poles in front and were in no mood to do drab jobs.) My client wanted me to wash a huge pile of dishes; she had given a party the night before. I contemplated the enormous heaps of greasy plates, glasses, cups, and pans. Ordinarily I'd have bowed out hastily. But I was a saint now. It took me two hours to clean up the mess while my client sat in a chair, scratched her head, groaned and remarked on her headache. "All that damn beer," she complained. "Four whole cases of it." I washed the dishtowels and hung them up, and cleaned up the sink. My client watched this with gratitude. "You're a swell kid," she said. "I'm going to give you fifteen cents instead of ten."

"Oh, no," I said, very, very gently, "I wouldn't take a penny. I was glad to do it for you."

Now there was usually a wrangle over proper payments: I always came out the winner. My client's mouth fell open and she stared at me, pop-eyed. "What did you say?" I repeated my saintly remark. She jumped to her feet. "You sick or something?" she demanded, terrified. "You coming down with something, and me with three kids?"

"No," I said, "it's just that I've changed."

She stared again, then put her hands to her head and staggered off to the bedroom. I heard the springs wail.

"Oh, God," she moaned, "I'm starting to hear things now!"

I stole delicately out of the house. Tommy, one of the fat slobs, yelled to me from halfway up the telephone post. "Yah! You can't climb this high! I climbed higher than you did, Friday!"

Climbing telephone poles was absolutely forbidden, and naturally I always climbed them with remarkable agility. But not today. The pole was seductive, but I shook my head. "I don't do those things any more, Tommy" I said, in my rich and unctuous tones. "And you shouldn't do them, either. Your mother doesn't like it."

"You're just scared," said Tommy triumphantly. But with a high head I went to my next client, the boy's cat-calls following me. On previous days I'd have returned, pulled him down off the pole and beaten him up. But not now. Ah, not now.

My next client was forbidden to me. I was never to speak to her, look at her, walk near her. I was only to ignore her existence. She was the neighborhood Scandal. But she paid twice as much as my other clients so I always sneaked in her back door to do her odd jobs for her. She was good for delicious slices of cake, too, and root beer, and she was exceedingly kind to children and actually liked them.

I did not know what made her so reprehensible, of course, but I had gathered from the whispers on porches that it had something to do with Men. Well, Papa was a man, and there were men in all the houses, and there was nothing about them very menacing and many things which were boring and dull. But I had noticed that every man, including Papa, always sent a furtive glance at my client's porch; and if they saw her they would give her a lurking smile, bend their heads and scurry home to their colorless wives. I had come to the conclusion that my client was a scandal because she was beautiful and gay, sang like an angel, dressed like a dream, and laughed a great deal; and perhaps I was not too wrong at that.

At any rate my client was married. Her husband was a quick little salesman with an apparently good income, for he dressed nattily, carried a cane, and often had a rosebud in his lapel. He also had an automobile; the only one for miles around. He traveled. He and I had one thing in common: We both adored his young wife. Sometimes, when I worked for her, he was at home. He would sit in their small gracious parlor, just watching her, smiling and smiling. Occasionally I would find her sitting in his lap embracing him with ardor, and the room perfumed with roses. It was a delightful vision, and it would give me joy to watch them—they were so young and happy and they had an innocence which was beguiling to a seven-year-old girl who, according to Papa, was "always up to one damn thing or another."

My client was alone at least five days and nights a week. Sometimes, late at night when I had stolen from the house to sit on the steps of the porch while my parents snored upstairs, I would see a gentleman walk quickly and silently into my client's house. I would see a light go on in my client's bedroom, and it would go off again. I never saw any gentleman leave. This was of no interest to me at all. I never caught a glimpse of their faces, but I did observe that they wore exceptionally fine clothes and that they often carried little boxes in their hands, or a sheaf of flowers. I would forget them instantly, and resume my happy contemplation of the night, at peace because there was no one else around and I was alone under the moon and in the shadow of thick trees. Sleepy at last, I would steal quietly back into my house, say my prayers, and go to bed.

On the Day I Was Absolutely Perfect my client was pleased to see me. Her rosy face was sparkly with dimples, and she appeared to be very happy. She wore a fascinating blue dress, trimmed with lace. She wanted me to polish her parlor floor, which gleamed always like glass. But first, as it was a warm spring day, she insisted that I have a slice of apple pie and a cup of coffee. We never had any coffee in our house, being British, and my parents disdained this "Yankee custom." Of course, I loved coffee. My client beamed at me while I ate an extra slice of pie. "Are you all right, dear?" she asked in her sweet voice, and she regarded me with solicitude. "You look different, somehow."

"Oh, I am," I assured her in my new rich tones. "I've decided to be a saint."

This jolted her. She stopped smiling and stared at me earnestly. Then she said, "You'll miss a lot of fun that way." It was evident she had fun all the time, she was always in such a lyrical state.

"I'm not interested in fun any more," I said. I was very grave. There are Covenanters far back somewhere in my family, and they all spoke through me at once. My client was even more jolted. "A little girl like you!" she cried, aghast. "Have your parents been beating you?"

According to my client all children were rather sacred, and, when punished by their exasperated parents, they were "beaten." In the past I had encouraged these misguided ideas of hers; they were good for cookies, a few chocolates, and an extra dime. Or once, happy day! a white little handkerchief dipped in perfume which I kept with me for weeks until I lost it. But I could not let my client be deceived any longer. "I only get strapped when I deserve it," I said, righteously.

My client was immediately depressed. She peeped at me uncertainly. "Oh, dear," she murmured. "How melancholy."

I wondered what I had said that was now making her look joyless and a little miserable. (I've seen since then, the exact expression on the faces of unfortunates being administered to lovingly and eagerly by dedicated workers and uplifters.) I went into her parlor, stuffed up to the ears with goodies, and began to polish her floor. I liked to do it; she was always so appreciative. She hovered in the doorway, today, restlessly, as if full of uneasiness and doubt and disquiet. (Any social worker knows that restlessness; they call it "guilt feelings" or loss of "self-worth.") My client wandered away. I finished up the job quickly, phrasing my words for rejection of payment. Then the door opened and a gentleman came in, all smiles and hope. "Angie!" he called.

My client came running and rustling into the parlor. She looked at me, then paled. The Gentleman saw me for the first time. "What's that kid doing, Angie?" he asked, disagreeably.

"Oh, George!" she exclaimed in distress. "You shouldn't have come—during the day!"

"But Angie, I have something wonderful to tell you, and I can't come tonight," he protested, and he took her hand and led her away. They went upstairs, murmuring. I had polished the floor. Now I dusted and wiped the fine little Dresden figurines in the cabinet. I did some more saintly work, not usually on my agenda. The back door opened and then closed, and my client came into the parlor. She started when she saw me, and I told her of the extra tasks I had done. Again she peeped at me, then put her arm about my neck and kissed me. "Here is fifty cents for you, darling," she said.

"No," I said, calmly, "I was glad to do it for you. I've changed!"

I almost faltered. Fifty cents! I ran from the house, exultant that I was running from temptation.

Then I saw Charley. Charley was a chunky, red-headed boy, mean as sin, a bully, and a spoiled monster. He was two years older than I, and I hated him. I don't remember why children hate without adequate reason. But Charley and I were sworn enemies and we never saw each other without a boxing match. Papa, like most British men, believed that girls should be trained athletically, as well as boys, and among other things he had taught me the manly art of self-defense. I was good at it. My fights with Charley almost always ended in a draw, though he won occasionally, as I did.

Upon seeing me now he doubled up his fists, went into a crouch and screamed, "Put 'em up!" I lusted for a fight with him. I licked my lips, clenched my hands, and advanced. Then I remembered that I was now a saint.

"Go away," I said loftily, and dropped my own fists. "I don't want to fight any longer."

Charley was stunned. "You crazy or somethin'?" he demanded, incredulous.

I scorned to answer, but did not scorn to watch him warily as I walked off. But Charley was too dazed to pursue or even utter another word. I had won another battle with self. This one didn't taste too good, but I reminded myself that I was now holy. I kept reminding myself all the way home. It was lunch-time and Papa was already at the table. "Well," he said, a little surlily, "how much did you scrounge this time? You ought to be ashamed."

"I worked, but I didn't take a cent," I said, giving Mama an angelic smile which made her step back hastily.

Papa snorted. "You mean, you didn't work," he said. I sat down in silence, patient and long-suffering. Mama, extraordinarily quiet, put a lamb chop before me. This was always a signal for a howl from me, for I loathed the things. But I daintily took up my knife and fork and began to eat the chop. I pushed every nauseating morsel down my throat. My parents watched me. Mama's mashed potatoes were always full of lumps and tasted like cold starch, but I ate them too without protest. I even ate the infernal damp carrots. My parents were fascinated. Once or twice they glanced at each other, mutely.

"Well!" said Mama at last, in a faint voice, and she sank into a chair. Papa, shaking his head, went back to his studio.

"I'll wheel Sonny around in his cart this afternoon, Mama," I said. "After I've washed up the dishes."

"What's wrong?" asked Mama, a little roughly. "What's come over you today? What've you been up to?"

"I worked, Mama," I said in a sugary voice. I paused. I had also disobeyed Mama. I had worked for Angie. Ah, no matter. So I heroically told Mama. Her eyes began to snap with fury. I told her about the gentleman, and what he had said to my client. Mama's eyes stopped snapping.

Mama hated gossip and never gossiped; she said so, herself, frequently. I believed her, naturally. She leaned towards me and asked me quick little questions. Who was the gentleman? Had I ever seen him before? What did That Woman say to him; I was to repeat everything he had said and what she had said. I did. Mama was quite flushed. She even smiled a little. Then she remembered that I had disobeyed, and she clipped me once. But absently, as if thinking of something else.

I rubbed my smarting cheek while Mama smiled faintly and somewhat maliciously. She became aware of me again. "Oh, that creature!" she said at last. "If there were any decency among people someone would tell her poor husband. This has gone too far. In the day, of all times! Has she no shame at all?"

I considered these remarks. I hadn't the slightest idea why my client should have any shame, but apparently it was expected of her. It was also expected that her husband be informed of the gentleman. Thinking these thoughts I took my brother out in his cart after I had washed the dishes. For some reason or other—and Mama was never a neighborhood visitor—she had gone to see the lady next door, in great haste.

Wheeling my brother was no fun. I would often relieve the monotony by giving the cart a hard shove down-street, then race it to the corner where I'd grab the handlebars just in time to keep my darling little kinsman from hurtling over the curb, and into the path of traffic. I had begun the preliminary warm-up when I remembered once more that I was a saint, and saints did not endanger the lives of little brothers, no matter how detestable. They definitely did not race and show their drawers to the public. I sauntered sedately with the cart and resolutely stifled my solid hate for small boys in general and my brother in particular.

Bored, I began to think again of Angie who was such a scandal, and the gentleman, and again of my mother's remark. I became excited. I would do another good deed, if Angie's husband returned that day. I wheeled Sonny's cart near her house, and walked it up and down. I doggedly paced, refusing an offer to play baseball and abandon Sonny on some lawn, refusing other offers to go skating. I was full of duty and thoughts and saintliness. I yawned, while keeping an eye on Angie's house, and I even brought myself to wipe Sonny's wet little nose. I usually let him drip, and at this time of the year he always dripped.

Then, to my joy, I saw Angie's husband coming up the street, his eyes already bright with love and anticipation. I pushed the go-cart rapidly towards him, and stopped him. He, like Angie, loved children, and he looked at me affectionately and this was remarkable as I was not a very attractive child. "I have something to tell you!" I told him, breathlessly, my heart swelling with goodness.

And so I told him.

He stopped smiling; he turned very white. His eyes looked sick. He kept wetting his mouth as he looked at me intently. Suddenly, he was not so very young any longer. He sagged a little. I continued my story, righteously. I told of the nightly visits of other gentlemen. "Mama says it is a scandal," I informed him, "She called your wife that Creature."

Then he spoke, very quietly. "And before a child, too." He patted me on my holy head and went slowly, slowly, up the street to his house. "Where's the automobile today?" I called after him. But he did not answer. His back was the back of an old man.

(I don't know what happened after that. I heard only fragments of remarks from my mother, and others. But Angie's husband was never seen again after that day. A few days later a pallid and weeping Angie left, after the furniture was taken out of the house and carted away. I was sorry to see her go, as I watched at a distance. She was a scandal, Mama had said, but I had liked her so much.)

I had done a terrible mischief in all innocence, and with only the most saintly of intentions. It was many years before I realized the fearful misery I had brought to two young people. Angie was doubtlessly a joyous sinner, but I had destroyed her husband's life and her own. She had been lovely and kind, and she really adored her husband and in time, losing her first youthful excitement over living, and coming to her senses, it is very possible that she would have reformed and have devoted her later years to a large family of children. After all, tens of thousands of quieted Magdalenes sleep in the hearts of multitudes of good wives and mothers. If only, I have often thought, I had not been a saint on that particular day, and full of urges to commit Good Deeds!

And now I also reflect on the evil crimes being committed these days against mankind everywhere by those moved by the utmost good-will and a firm determination to reform and change human nature. I ponder on the rage they must evoke, and the terror and despair and ruin and anguish. The do-gooders may, as I was, be anxious only to be helpful; they may even devote all their lives to a dubious duty, and with selflessness. They may think they are assisting man to a higher estate. They may, in reality, be assisting him to Hell, as Angie and her husband were so assisted; and with the same innocence. Talleyrand said, "It is not enough to do good. It is often better to refrain from doing good, judiciously." Every seasoned clergyman learns that.

Oh, what happened to my saintliness? I forgot all about it the following morning because the first day had ended in total boredom and with an inner sensation of emptiness. "It was too good to last," said my father, gloomily, (but with some relief), when I came in the next day with a bloody nose after an exhilarating boxing-match with Charley, which I had won, and a pocketful of nickels and dimes.

I have never been a "saint" since, though often tempted. My guardian angel hastily helps me change my mind. And so I have not committed any other mischief, either, as I did on the Day I Was Absolutely Perfect.

4

Sharing

It was a Monday morning and Teacher smiled at us radiantly. (It did seem to cause her pain, but never mind.) She said, "Children, we are going to play a new game today! We call it "Sharing Our Week-End Experiences." That means you will all take turns telling all the rest of us what wonderful things happened to you on Saturday and Sunday, and what you did and thought, and where your parents took you, and what you said, and what you played. Won't that be fun!"

We kids stared at Teacher vacantly, and blinked. The old girl continued to beam at us encouragingly. Then she pointed to a little boy; "Tommy dear; Do tell us what *you* did this wonderful spring week-end! And what your mama and papa talked about!" She had a notebook open and a pen poised.

Tommy rose sluggishly and blinked. "Well, uh," he said. "Saturday I skated. Sunday, we went to church. We, uh, had a big dinner. We all went to sleep. Then we went to the park and watched the airplane over the river. We came home and had some sandwiches, and then we went to bed."

Teacher wrote rapidly. "And what did you think about it all?" she cried.

Tommy considered. "I wished school was out. I wished it was summer, so I wouldn't have to go to school no more."

Teacher's pen flew. Her face became serious. She said, "Don't you like school, Tommy?"

Now, it is normal for healthy children to despise school with all their barbarian little hearts, and even young children suspect those mates who declare they "love" school. They consider them either liars or fools out trying to attract the favor of Teacher. They are quite right, of course, and a thorough dislike for school was once accepted as quite natural among teachers, who probably hated it, too. But Teacher had been taught that a child was "in emotional difficulties" if he didn't like being tied to a desk all day and confined in a dreary space, while the sun shone outside invitingly.

"I hate school!" said Tommy, with powerful emotion, and we almost applauded.

Teacher's face was now really somber. She made several more notes, then called on a little girl. The child's recital was dull. So were the ones following. An ominous sleepiness began to overpower me. A delicious inertia was creeping over me, and a soft darkness, when Teacher's voice sharply awakened me. "Janet Caldwell! It is your turn to share."

I stood up, crumpled as always, with my red hair over my face and in my eyes. I considered. The other kids had had uneventful week-ends, all seriously the same, and all tepid. Mine *could* have been gloriously different. Still, I hesitated. The British indoctrination of reticence had been pounded well into me at home and in British schools. Teacher fixed me with her hypnotic eye. "Well, well?"

she said, with impatience. "Surely something happened at home, Janet, over the week-end that you can share with us."

Kids, as a rule, have a pathetic belief in the omniscience of adults. I hadn't as yet discarded that belief, though it had begun to waver alarmingly when I was three. So, I considered that if Teacher wanted to know my experience it was quite all right to crank up a really good one for her. Hadn't I been taught that one was to obey one's superiors?

In the two weeks I had been in that school I had already acquired a little notoriety among my innocent playmates, so that the half-dozing class came to attention and stared at me. This was both flattering and unnerving, but children love an audience. I brought the week-end experience into my inner eye and suddenly found it quite exciting, far different from the memoirs of my fellow-sufferers.

"On Saturday afternoon," I said, "Mama almost brained Papa with a frying pan, and then she threw a knife at him, and then he want out to the saloon and got drunk and didn't come home until Sunday morning. He didn't look well. He had a black eye. He told Mama it was worth it, and she hit him again. With the rolling pin, this time."

My schoolmates were enchanted. They laughed and clapped, and I preened. But Teacher was pale with horror. She said, in a hushed voice, "Your parents used violence on each other, Janet?"

I wasn't too certain what violence meant, but the sound of it seemed to fit the case. I nodded happily. "But Mama can hit harder," I informed the class, who applauded again (especially the little girls). "Mama can hit *very* hard," I went on, "though she's little. Papa's afraid of her, though sometimes he hits back."

Teacher folded her hands prayerfully on the desk. The kids looked at me with envy. What had their week-ends been in comparison with mine? Dullsville.

"Was your mother . . . er, drunk—too?" asked Teacher, almost whispering.

I considered. Now I come of two hard-drinking races and never will I lie and say that liquor never crossed Mama's lips. I didn't lie then, either. "Oh, Mama drinks, too," I said airily. "But I don't think they get drunk. They don't fall on the floor, like the men I see coming out of the saloons sometimes. They just fight."

I am sure I made a Prohibitionist of Teacher on the spot. She closed the notebook as if it were the Book of Doom, and rested her hand upon it and gently bit her lip. She stared into space. She said, "Spelling books, children."

That was a come-down, of course. Later, Teacher asked me, in a hushed voice, to remain a few minutes after school. This was annoying. Mama had no patience with tardiness, and I had to wheel little Brother in the afternoons, and Mama took no excuses. After the other kids had left the room at two-thirty, Teacher drew me tenderly and slowly to her knee and gazed deeply and compassionately into my eyes.

"Tell me, dear," she said, "did you cry and tremble when your mother—did what she did to your father?"

I was astonished. "No," I said, "I thought she had killed Papa, at first." I was a little regretful. Not that I didn't have great affection for Papa, but murder is dramatic and children are eager for drama.

Teacher had begun to scribble in her notebook again, and for the first time a little apprehension touched me. Her pen was quite feverish. She said, "Janet, dear, didn't you just *shake* when you thought your Mama had killed your Papa?"

I thought this over, trying to remember. Hazy remembrance came to me. "Oh, I thought if she'd killed him he might be hanged, or something. Then he got up off the couch."

"Dear sweet Heaven," breathed Teacher. Her eyes were

full of tears. She helped me on with my coat, something no adult had done since I had been three, and she took my hand and said bravely, "We really must talk to Mama."

Now apprehension rose to fear. I tried to pull my hand away. "Mama will *kill* me!" I exclaimed. Alas, as always, prudence came to me too late. And tears. I yelled with fright, seeing Mama's outraged face. "You made me tell the class!" I screamed at Teacher, "I didn't want to, but you made me!"

I had visions of police, and me in prison, iron doors clanging after me. Teacher had somehow pervaded my mind with criminality as well as terror. What had I done? I suddenly knew—too late, as usual—that Mama would not look kindly on my breach of reticence to entertain the class. How could I have forgotten that before my parents did battle they were careful to close doors and draw draperies?

I must have impressed Teacher with my terror, for she dived again for notebook and wrote something in it. This released my hand. I wanted to run for my life. And, believe me, I was sure it was my life. To this very moment the trauma of it remains with me; I never see Big Mommy in action or hear her voice in our suborned Press and on TV and in the mouths of politicians without that old feeling of sixty years ago, that feeling of imminent terror and despair, of absolute helplessness, and the desire to flee to some safe spot.

Teacher patted my shoulder. "All right, dear," she said. "Go home, alone. It will be all right." I fled, trembling and sweating with dread and with the sensation that I had escaped something terrible. I had. Temporarily.

We occupied an apartment on quite a nice street in my home city, and Mama had brought treasured family antiques with her from England, including some fine tables and mirrors and an excellent oriental rug or two. We also had beautiful lace curtains and velvet curtains, and Mama was a furious housekeeper, keeping everything shined and polished and scrubbed while she bewailed her lot in America not having a maid-of-all-work as she had had in England. And there was usually something very savory simmering on the stove, and the house smelled of wax and polish and lavender, and the windows glittered.

Home was a haven to me that afternoon, though usually it definitely was not—being filled with chores I had to do after my stroll with little Brother. I was very subdued and didn't once complain. Papa, home for tea, gazed at me apprehensively. "Is the lass ill?" he asked.

Mama roughly felt my brow. "She isn't feverish," she said. "She didn't cause me any trouble today, and that's unusual. Maybe I'd better give her a dose of castor oil and syrup of rhubarb, just to be certain."

To show my state of mind, I was even glad to take that horrible stuff, remembering Teacher and my narrow escape from catastrophe. But later that night a policeman came to the door and requested an interview with my parents. I looked at him with absolute terror, because I was filled with premonitions.

To the British, the police are sacrosanct, are Authority and are respected. That is, they were until comparatively recently. The Police did not come to one's house except under dire provocation. My parents were aghast. Here was the Law. He was also a big young Irishman with a fresh face, and he looked about our nice and shining apartment with puzzled astonishment. I know now that he had expected a filthy slum and broken cartons and dirt and drunkenness and, possibly, blood on the floor. His eye fell on me, and he saw me glaring with fright at him, and he pursed his lips. (I can see it all as vividly as if it were happening just now.) He cleared his throat. He was embarrassed.

Papa, with a very white face, invited him to sit down and Mama queried if he'd like a "nice cup of tea." Her little hands were trembling. The young policeman, recognizing an Irishman when he saw one, sat down and thanked Mama for the tea, and she added some pound cake and fresh cream. He stirred his cup and thoughtfully watched the swirls in it.

"I tell you, Mr. Caldwell," he said at last, "there's been prowlers around this neighborhood in the past couple weeks, and we're looking for them, and I thought maybe you'd seen them around. Nice flat like this. Just what they've been looking for." He admired the heavy silver teaspoon and weighed it in his hand.

Papa had heard that America was a violent country, long before he had come here, and so he was not surprised. He almost regretfully assured the policeman that he had seen no criminals.

"And a lot of *drunkenness* gets reported to us," said the young man. "Mean neighbors, I'll be thinking. A body can't take a drop anymore without some Nosy Parker calling the Po-lice."

Papa caught the drift at once, and so did Mama; but, thank God, they didn't connect it with me. They were indignant, and nodded their heads. "Mind my words," said Papa, darkly, "they'll be stopping us from having a drop of the Creature one of these days. Will you have a drop?"

The young policeman did. When he rose to go he considered me. "Nice little girl you have here, Mr. Caldwell," he said, in a voice which denied the words, and his look at me was stern. I was rescued.

5

The Purple Lodge

The nature of human beings never changes; it is immutable. The present generation of children and the present generation of young adults from the age of thirteen to eighteen is, therefore, no different from that of their great-great-grandparents. Political fads come and go; theories rise and fall; the scientific "truth" of today becomes the discarded error of tomorrow. Man's ideas change, but not his inherent nature. That remains. So, if the children are monstrous today—even criminal—it is not because their natures have become more polluted, but because they have not been taught better, nor disciplined.

When I was nine years, I became part of a gangster group in my school. There were fourteen of us; I believe we called ourselves the Purple Lodge because some of the children had Masonic fathers who went to lodges. Anyway, it had a rich and terrible sound and children healthily love anything that smacks of violence. One of the reasons that we formed the gang was because we were bored to death in school, and normally healthy and intelligent youngsters usually are—despite what the "educationists" try to tell parents.

Our lodge met in the basement of the school, behind the smelly coal furnaces, once a week, and with the connivance of the janitor we built ourselves a sort of shed to give us an illusion of a cave and secrecy. We had passwords and secret gestures which we used in school to the bafflement of our teacher, who unfortunately turned out to be too bright for us little criminals. But that was later.

Every week Walter, our leader, assigned each member of the Purple Lodge to a special project against authority both in school and at home. We all knew each other's assignment and we were vigilant.

One week Walter assigned me to start with the fourth floor and work down to the first, scribbling ribald words on every teacher's door-card, which bore her name and her classroom number. Walter gave me a big list of four-letter words, a list entirely unnecessary; for by the time a child is nine years old he or she knows nearly all of them anyway. Children acquire these things by osmosis, for the healthy and normal child is by nature rude and uncouth.

The reason this assignment had been given to me was because I was noted for being a fine printer, a fact I brought to Walter's attention. "They'll all know I did it," I said. (A member of the Lodge who was caught was automatically expelled from our wicked brotherhood.) Walter said, "Disguise it, then. Write it out instead of printing it. You have a clear hand." The assignment was dangerous, which made it all the more fascinating. You had to get to school earlier than the teachers or wait until after school when the teachers had gone, or you had to do it during recess or during a break for the lavatory. It was a ticklish matter. But I rose to the occasion nobly.

As I was fast on my feet and dexterous, and as sly as

the normal child, I was able to complete the fourth floor on the first day. By the end of the week the assignment was done. And the teachers, and the principal, were in an uproar. It was decided, of course, that the crime had been committed by a big boy, and certainly not by a little girl. Walter was pretty shrewd, you will discern, in choosing me.

The biggest boy in school, Sam, was in the ninth grade, and he had been frequently caught sending suggestive notes to little girls who had inspired his admiration and affection. He was not a member of the Lodge, of course. And he didn't know half the dirty words I did. But, as he had come under discipline for using the words he did know, suspicion fell on him immediately. The principal put into operation the machinery for expulsion in spite of poor Sam's despairing denials. Sam was a top student and an expert mathematician and his parents were in a position to send him to college. This black mark on his record, and the expulsion, would work an awful hardship on him, and besides it was unjust.

We had a conference behind the furnaces. No more than other children did we possess a sense of honor and a love for justice. But for several of us there was Confession, and we knew exactly what our confessors would tell us to do after the grim penances were assigned. All of us would be told to confess the name of the criminal to the authorities, in order to save Sam and to save our souls. This was a dilemma. The Lodge was also in danger. My assignment, it seems, had been the most audacious of them all and the most criminal.

Walter was a Protestant. He looked at me gloomily and said, "I shouldn't have picked any Catholics who'll go blabbering to the priest." For the benefit of those who don't know, I will explain that during Confession you hold nothing back nor have any mental reservations. Otherwise you don't get absolution, and we children firmly believed in Hell.

I was ready to brave Hell-fire, I assured them. This horrified Walter, a stern Baptist. Loyalty to members of the Lodge was an absolute must, and Walter could not even consider putting my immortal soul in jeopardy. Jail, yes. Punishment, yes. But not Hell-fire. As the leader, Walter made the decision. He would write an anonymous note to the principal saying that poor Sam was not guilty, that he knew the guilty person but would not blab. Walter ended up on a virtuous note, for naughty children know how to move adults' hearts: "We want only justice for Sam, for we are good children."

But it seems that some of my words had been exceptionally fruity and descriptive, so even the sentimentalists among the teachers could not assuage the just wrath of the principal. One of our spies told us gleefully that Dr. Smith had asserted that the criminal was "unusually depraved." The other members of the Lodge looked at me with added respect.

Finally, one teacher got wind of the Purple Lodge; we never knew who the betrayer was. She was certain that a member of our criminal brotherhood was guilty. Unfortunately, our own teacher had long had suspicions of Walter. She must have been abnormally shrewd, for Walter was an example of rectitude during school hours. Being intelligent, she suspected the well-behaved and apparently conforming. She came down on Walter. He never confessed. He never was a traitor. But his manner must have convinced the sharp-eyed dragon. She summoned his grim Germanic mother to the school. We all knew about Mrs. Schultz, from Walter's harrowing descriptions. She believed in discipline. She was similar to my own parents, and bore quite a resemblance to the parents of the others, too. But they never tried to put us out of business for more than a few hours, whereas Walter's mother believed in so dexterously punishing her offspring that they were *hors-de-combat* for a week.

Mrs. Walter Schultz arrived at ten o'clock on one dark

winter morning, a little woman as broad as she was tall, and solid muscle. Before all the children in the class she thoroughly beat up poor Walter, and even gave him a bloody nose. But no punishment would induce Walter to betray his fellow criminals. Silently, though tears ran down his cheeks, he incurred his misery and the powerful arm of his mother. We hated her with all our hearts and prayed for her sudden, violent, and painful death. We felt let down by God because she did not drop dead on the floor after preliminary writhings. Poor Walter was out of school for a day or two, but on his return we greeted him as a hero. He had never betrayed us.

Walter was also a hero during Wilson's War. He was decorated posthumously for valor on the battlefield, and he was only nineteen. I have never forgotten Walter.

Naturally, I do not believe in Mrs. Schultz's method of punishment. But I do believe in stern discipline, and no nonsense. I do believe in remembering that children are naturally infirm so far as acceptable virtue is concerned, and that they are not "delicate" and precious little blossoms as some of the child worshippers assert. Virtue in children, and civic responsibility, is something that must be taught painfully by stern parents and sterner teachers. Children do not come by it naturally, being human. A child starts out, even in these "loving" days, by having no more a sense of decency and kindness and charity and reverence than did his caveman ancestor. These are things which must be taught by strict discipline, example, and the power of a parent's good right arm.

The child psychologists, and the sentimental in general, disagree with me. A child, they assert, comes into the world absolutely pure, a saint in fact, uncorrupted, who does not inherit the savage instincts of his forebears. When I have told these silly creatures about the Purple Lodge they have looked shocked or disdainful. Children these days, they passionately affirm, are different. They arrive in an angelic condition, unpolluted and immaculate. They are "naturally" full of eager love, willingness to cooperate and share, anxious for justice and peace, and beatific. Child lovers simply will not be realistic. And so they are deftly used by nasty children—and all children are born nasty and human, and reeking with Original Sin.

6

The Child-Lovers

The child-lovers had already arrived when I was an unregenerate kid. The schools began to be invaded by tender sentimentalists under the guidance of the school boards. They set up physical examination clinics in the schools—iodine and aspirin centers, really. Of course, a lot of children, especially the brighter ones, took advantage of this marvelous situation. The child-lovers, who believed that young children are incapable of dissimulation, were easily hoodwinked. The child-lovers severely told our teachers that if a child complained of a headache or a pain he must be sent home or to the school nurse, and his word invariably accepted. So, a lot of us, including me, had many happy, free days. We didn't go home, of course, after our compassionate dismissal with a note for our mothers "urging" immediate attention. We raced the streets, had informal picnics with our school lunches, skated, explored. And forged our mothers' signatures on the notes for the next day, or the next week. In the meantime our mothers remained ignorant of the fact that their kids were loose on the city. And the child-lovers never caught on, happily. We were The Children, and so beyond guile and normal human criminality. We were the Sanctified, and we never disputed it.

When I arrived in the seventh grade I, as well as the rest of the kids, was joyously aware of the new "loving" situation in school. A few days in September convinced me that Miss Jones was a terrible person. Not herself a child-lover, she used a ruler manfully on us. She also believed in learning and constant study. She would march up and down the aisle with her clever weapon, leaving a smarting wake behind her. This was intolerable. Moreover, as it was now the rule that "slow" children should be accommodated at the expense of the more intelligent, a lot of us were bored to death. We had already, in the first weeks of school, raced through our textbooks while the dumb kids were still painfully on the beginning ten pages. So, we used the child-lovers to escape school, in spite of Miss Jones' eminently intelligent statements that we were born liars and not to be trusted for a moment. Happily, the child-lovers did not believe her; they regarded her as "reactionary."

By the middle of October, I was fed up with Miss Jones and her medieval ideas that children were creatures of sin and needed to be restrained. So I decided on the normal course of action, with the help of the child-lovers. I developed a Heart Condition. I was a great student of Mama's many medical books and I had the symptoms down pat.

Mama, of course, was a skeptic. I started with Mama so she would not be unduly suspicious when I was relieved of school. I began to complain of vague pains in the region of my still unbusted chest, and breathlessness. When I approached the house I stopped running and skating. I removed the skates. I wandered into the house listlessly, and sat down, breathing unevenly and gaspingly. I had decided that a rheumatic heart condition was the best; it was quite common among children in those days and it would be regarded with less doubt than, say, a coronary occlusion or a stroke. I told Mama that a few weeks ago I had a "terrible" sore throat. As I had enlarged tonsils anyway—the subject of much anxious flurrying among the child-lovers—the sore throat gambit did not needlessly arouse Mama's cynicism. I was always having sore throats. Mama was hard to convince, though. She did not relieve me of my household chores though she did buy me iron tonics. I was naturally white of skin and could use this physical characteristic to good advantage with the child-lovers who thought all pale children starving or ill or physically abused by "unloving and rejecting parents."

Then I had a "heart attack" right in the midst of mathematics lesson, which I naturally detested. It was a fine one, too; I was a wonderful actress. I was immediately sent down to Dr. Smith and the school nurse, though Miss Jones heartlessly refused to accompany me. As no child-lover will ever expect a child to be a liar and a faker, the school nurse threw her arms about me tearfully and knelt before my bony knees, embraced me, and began to question me. The principal, Dr. Smith, was a little harder to convince, he having had too much experience with the children over the years. But I was a match even for him. I had all the authentic symptoms. I knew enough not to exaggerate. I let the story of my symptoms be dragged from me, piteously, and with an air of total childish innocence. I made my eyes big and apprehensive and moved them from face to face, in the meanwhile gulping pathetically. The nurse pointed out to Dr. Smith that I had the fragile bluish appearance of a heart patient. So far so good.

"Do you get enough to eat, darling?" asked the tearful nurse.

Mama's cooking was deplorable, but there were platters of it and all of it had to be devoured at one sitting. As we were British we had meat three times a day, and so I naturally loathed meat.

I whimpered, "I love fish, but we get it only on Fridays."

The nurse was convinced that I was underfed, for I was also tall for my age and skinny. My father, the nurse was sure, could afford proteins for us only on Fridays. She began to make notes, and I carefully and quickly read the notes out of the corner of my wicked eye. "Insufficent proteins," she wrote. "Conducive to heart strain, as well as to rheumatic fever?"

And so it went. By the time the examination was completed I definitely had had rheumatic fever, was starved at home because of insufficient income on the part of my father, and was "severely disciplined by parents and so rendered timid, fearful and insecure."

The discipline at home was quite correct, but I was hardly timid, fearful or insecure.

Tenderly, I was dismissed for the day and roared joyously out into the invigorating October sunshine. I went to a far-off park where I contentedly devoured my huge lunch and drank my milk. I had a wonderful thing going. I contemplated months of complete freedom from Miss Jones, and mathematics, and the dull children. All was ecstasy. I pitied my mates that they did not possess my astuteness and so had to attend school.

I had overlooked disaster, of course.

When I arrived home at the usual hour—there was no sense in trying to draw Mama into the conspiracy—I opened the door to discover that the school nurse was seated in the kitchen protesting to Mama, who was not only baffled but furiously angry. On my entry, the nurse held out her protecting arms to me but Mama caught me by the shoulder and exclaimed, "What devilment have you been up to now?" This gesture, I saw with pleasure, horrified the school nurse. Mama followed up the grasp with a smart hand slap in my lying face. I burst into shrieks. The nurse ran to rescue me. "Don't, don't!" she sobbed at Mama. Mama was unaccustomed to me shrieking, and she fell back, the very picture of guilt.

Then Mama pulled herself together. "The little liar is starved, is she?" she demanded. "She needs more proteins, does she? Come here, you," she said to the nurse and banged open the oven door to show the eight-rib roast beef cooking there, savory in its juices and surrounded by browning onions, carrots and potatoes. "I bet you," Mama said to the nurse, "you never see such a roast like this more than once or twice a year, and then only on a holiday. And look at this ox-tail soup! Stiff with barley and vegetables, and look at this apple pie! When did you eat such a meal last, and this is what we have all the time!"

The nurse was stunned. She looked pleadingly at me for denial, but I dared not deny for Mama's black eyes were sparkling ominously. "She eats like a horse," Mama went on. "She'll eat half this pie herself, and ask for more. And she gets at least a quart of milk a day, too. Like a horse."

"Maybe fish?" whispered the nurse. "She loves fish."

"Does she?" cried Mama. "Who told you that? She'll eat only smoked herring, and turns up her nose at halibut and trout. So I've been getting herring just for her, and all those Norwegian sardines. A pampered brat, that's all."

But the nurse, though shattered, was still convinced that I was Only an Innocent Child. She also had authority. She left Mama a notice that I was not to return to school until I had had a complete physical examination, especially for my heart. The house was tensely silent that night. I tiptoed around and did my homework meekly.

I had never had a doctor in my life up to then, and neither had my parents. Doctors were a Yankee fetish, and only "encouraged" people to be sick in order to fatten their purses. But Mama marched me off to a doctor the next day, and her hand was painfully clenched on my arm.

As I had fearfully expected, the doctor assured Mama that I was not only sound in limb and wind and muscle, but had an excellent heart and no signs of any rheumatic fever. "What an imagination the child has," said the doctor admiringly. But Mama did not admire me. The visit had cost two dollars.

Mama took me home and expertly pounded the hell out of me, and Papa enthusiastically carried on the job. I went back to school the next day, and to rigorous servitude under Miss Jones. She was especially stern with me, for good reason. I had almost deceived her. But she was pleased that the child-loving nurse had been bilked. "Not that that will teach such people a lesson," said Miss Jones. "Delicate, fragile, innocent children! My eye!"

My eye, indeed.

I warned my nefarious pals at school that faking illness to escape school was not the best of ideas, considering skeptical mothers. I was a prime example.

Children have not changed. And they are still wickedly clever. They fervently agree with the new doctrine that they are innocent flowers, pure and uncorrupted and piteous, the prey of heartless adults. (I know, my own children tried the trick, but remembering my youthful days I was not deceived.) So in concert with the child-lovers they are getting away with wholesale murder in our schools. Discipline is now unknown. The spanking of children is criminal, the child-lovers assert, and so no teacher these days dares even to defend herself against hulking "children" in their teens. The schools are in total chaos. The homes are terrified by monsters whose will is not to be denied lest they acquire some "trauma" of the spirit.

And society, the courts, the judges, the social workers, are now the hosts and servants of idiot child-psychiatrists. Is there any wonder, then, that such an alarming number of crimes in America are now committed by undisciplined young people under the age of eighteen? Terrible crimes, too, including murder and assaults, drunkenness, and drug-addiction? Is there any wonder that our children are wild, undisciplined, evil and incorrigible, and full of socialistic doctrines? They have been taught that the world is theirs, and theirs only, and that there is no reason for them to restrain themselves, nor to learn to honor authority and to love God and country.

No one, of course, is convinced that society is in need of protection from our terrible offspring, the result of our secular, "loving" education and the sick pampering they receive in our homes. We are reaping the harvest of our own weaknesses. It is a frightful one.

When I survey the present scene I am not only appalled, but I thank God that my parents were tough. I wish to God there were tens of millions of parents in America just like them! Unless we soon have them, we are done for as a nation.

Take a hard look at your children. If they are five or older set them to work in your houses after school and on Saturday. See that they are well employed on Sundays at church, and in the house, and finishing up homework. By the time they are ten they should be doing gainful work in the neighborhood at something or other. When they reach puberty, tell them they are no longer children but are young adults. They should be working after school somewhere, to take up all that free time they have. Inspect their schools and talk harshly to the children-lovers. Talk harshly to the School Boards, too. Study your clergyman, and remove your family from his influence if he is all for the Social Gospel, and find a man who talks of the Eternal Verities. Teach them that this world is only a way-station to eternity and time is precious and not for "fun." Teach them to be men and women in the real world. Be tough!

Do all this, unless you prefer the coming barbarism and the long night of death and misery. It has happened to other nations in the past, nations like ourselves, and it will happen to us. It is your choice. After all, you let America get into this condition. Now, help her get out.

7

Learning the Liberal Lingo

Suppose you want to "get along" with Liberals for the sake of your job or your career.

I have some suggestions, whereby you can "pass."

It is probably best to begin by memorizing a few all-important phrases for when you talk to Liberals. And do make your voice softly sing when repeating them. You don't have to be mentally present when you do. You can think about your taxes, the high cost of living, new diapers for the baby, the upcoming mortgage payment, the intransigence of your boss or your employees, the fact that your husband/wife doesn't understand you, the inexplicable ways of your teenagers, the umbrageousness of your clergyman, the necessity for taking down/putting up the storm-windows and screens, how to meet your installment payments, how to get a loan, how to get rid of that crabgrass in your lawn. These can occupy your mind for several hours when conversing with your Liberal friends, and you can have a fine time while repeating clichés.

Remember, though, speak softly. Now, all together: "Underprivileged, disadvantaged, culturally deprived." "Participation, integration, desegregation, cooperation." Liberals love involved words. If you can think up some more utterly meaningless ones, all to the good. The less meaning there is in words the more Liberals love them. Never use words of one syllable. You might study the dictionary for multi-meaning words, the more erotic the better. If the Liberal doesn't understand them—and you don't have to, either—he will consider you an intellectual, and you have now captured him. Try charismatic, and opt, and hubris. Don't bother looking them up. Just use them.

Use psychiatric words, the more esoteric the more approved. Try involution, delivered with a grave expression. Or inter-personal, related, outgoing, other-directed, Id, supra-conscious, inverted, ruminative. For a more earthy touch casually speak of the "traumatic results of too-early toilet-training." That gets the Liberal where he lives.

Just listen to the younger ones talk of "under-achievement" and "over-achievement," and "striving to conform to the peer group," and "personal involvement in intra-personal relationships on the mundane levels." If the Liberals are Catholic, speak of Teilhard de Chardin and the noosphere. (No, I don't know what that means!) Speak of Man-Becoming and Christ-Becoming and Supra-Man and Supra-Christ. If the Liberals are Protestants, speak of the Social Gospel. (Liberal Catholics like that, too.) If of the Jewish faith, you can win them over by talking of "ingrained anti-Semitism," and "the role religion has played in modern anti-Semitism." During this conversation put on an expression of delicate horror and regret. It isn't necessary to be totally conscious during this time. The Liberal won't be aware that you are irrelevant (another fine word). He will just recognize the passwords, and nod approvingly.

Talk of Black Power, and Le Roi Jones: at this point it is wise to bow the head as if in guilt and waiting for a deserved lash because of your many sins. The more guilty you look, the more moved, the more repentant—the more the Liberal will love you and call you "sensitive." But in your emotion, utter a four-letter word now and then—as if you are unbearably touched and stirred and are forced to explode in your righteous wrath, though regretting the outburst. Then you have him in your pocket. Control yourself if he reaches over to you and murmurs consolingly and strokes your arm. You have to put up with this if you want the approval of your Liberal friend, or at the very least turn aside his hatred. His hatred is nothing to laugh at; it can be most dangerous.

Speak of "the complex problems of our modern world," and "no simplistic solution." It doesn't matter that the world of men has always been complex and that there has never been any simple solution for the crimes committed by men, world without end. Just indicate to the Liberal that you believe this is an entirely new world, requiring an entirely new philosophy, new solutions, and new answers. The word "new" can even stand alone, although the *Holy Bible* repeatedly says, "There is nothing new under the sun." Speak contemptuously of "old, outmoded values."

Speak of the "irrelevance of God in this modern world." Casually mention that "God is dead." Some Liberal churchgoers may wince a little, if faith isn't entirely dead with them, but they will acknowledge that you are "bold," anyway, and that's what you want, isn't it? They will even look gravely tolerant and remark that though they may not entirely agree with you, "you do have a point." But shy away if they ask you to elaborate. You can't—but you can wave your hand wearily and give the impression that in this intellectual company it surely isn't necessary for you to enlarge on the subject.

The old-line Liberal is a hypocrite when it comes to sex

and natural functions. Repeat that at least five times, and
write it on your brain. He is repelled by the idea of blad-
ders and bowels and the less attractive aspects of the
human body, and he is scared to death of disease, being
by nature a hypochondriac of the most awesome kind. (If
he has a pet disease, it is all right to talk of that briefly and
with sympathy.) But the Liberal loves to talk of Sex, and
the less potent he is the more he delights in "sex drives
and imperatives." He wants details, too, and leans avidly
forward to hear you expound on your sex life and drives.
Now you've got yourself boxed in if you aren't careful.
Edge away from the proximity of your spouse, who might
become too interested—and drift away to a corner with
your Liberal friend, and indicate that you "know exactly
what you mean . . . but in this company . . ." Look elo-
quent. The Liberal will gather that you mean you are both
intellectuals in the company of Philistines who "won't
understand," and he will touch your arm fondly. Sigh at
this point; drop your head and shake it dolorously. Wander
away, with an aspect of grief. He will follow you sadly
with his eyes if you are lucky. Stay away from him the rest
of the evening. Try to explain to your spouse. This will
take some doing, if you are overheard.

If you are among Liberals who are also parents, you can
speak of the "sex drives of the pre-teen years." You didn't
of course, have much of a sex drive when you were a pre-
teen, even though you were normally curious about What
Goes On. But indicate to the Liberal that you were a posi-
tive satyr, or at least a nymph or a Lolita, depending on
your sex. Perversion is absolutely fascinating to the Liberal. Look to the movies of Hollywood, for instance, and
some of the books the Liberals write. Your Liberal pal
may even have trifled with perversion, and righteously
speak of "sex in any form between consenting adults."
Don't ask him to give details! Speak about the "new
sexual revolution," as if you had never heard of Sodom
and Gomorrah, where the new sexual revolution was in

full flower before God did smite them with fire and brim-
stone. But you can mention the ancient Greeks, with a
wise smile. The Liberal may know nothing of history, but
he sure has heard of the ancient Greeks and what they were
up to!

Look up a few exotic terms for sexual perversion in
psychiatric books, if you intend to be at home with sophisticated Liberals. They may make you gag, but be brave
and learn them. And speak them when necessary.

After all, some Liberal may have a fat order he can
give you for your widgets, or he may know an industrialist
whom he has corrupted and has in his pocket. You are all
for unrestricted trade, aren't you, and getting along with
people? Or, if the Internal Revenue Service is at present
unduly interested in your books, the Liberal may mention
—after a meaningful conversation with you on this and
that—that he "knows" a little chap right down there in
the Service. After all, you are one of the boys, or girls
aren't you? You are right up there With It. Later you may
reflect, but if you are of sturdy stuff you will shrug and
say to yourself, "That's the way the cookie crumbles." A
good syrup to soothe a coughing conscience. But that's the
way the world is. Is it your fault? Did you make this
world? The fact that you helped make it can be ignored
—for a little while, until you are alone with yourself.
Then a couple of stiff barbiturates help, or a handful of
tranquilizers. Or half a dozen shots of bourbon.

It's eminently desirable in these days to denounce the
War in Vietnam when among Liberals. Denounce all war;
talk of "sensible men coming to practical solutions." Of
course, *never, but never,* denounce World War II. That
was a Holy War, beloved of the Liberals. They have
called it, in my presence, "a lovely war." They adored
it. They even have excuses for the atomic bombing of
those two defenseless Japanese cities. "It saved American
lives." You know that is a lie, but don't nail the liar. Bad
business. Just sigh. If you were in F.D.R.'s war, mention

the girls in London and Paris and make out that you were a sly dog, indeed, up to your ears in constant sex. If you were a bomber, tell how glorious it was to bomb the open and undefended city of Dresden in the closing days of that war, and how nice it felt to kill a quarter of a million little children and nuns and women on the streets of Dresden at the beginning of Lent, 1945. "Just retribution," say it with righteousness. But—be sure to bewail, with open tears if possible, the inadvertent killing of North Vietcong villagers by napalm and bombs. Talk of "barbarism." It was one thing to kill the wives and babies of German soldiers. It is quite a different thing to kill the wives and babies of the kindly Communist Vietcong. Don't ask me why. Am I a Liberal? You just have to live with these things, if you don't want a Liberal as your deadly enemy.

Praise Senator Fulbright for his "humane dissent." But never, never, ask if Senator Fulbright denounced Roosevelt's War! That is putting the Liberals on the spot, and that's where they hate to be. Remember: It was one thing to kill Nazis. It is another thing to kill Communists. The one was righteous. The second, heinous. Never forget!

Earnestly assure your Liberal pal that though you are not a Communist, "one has to understand their point of view in these complex days." The Liberal will assure you that he, too, has no use for the Communists. Then tell him you don't believe for a moment that the riots in our northern cities were inspired by white Communists rousing up the unfortunate black people. He will heartily agree with you.

If you are a lady Conservative and don't want to get a bad reputation for speaking the truth, your natural comic arts will help you better than acting will help your husband. Very few men are good actors; women are born actresses. A woman can smile even when she is lusting for your guts, and so a woman can easily deceive even the most perceptive of Liberals, providing they are male.

(Not so easy with the lady "Liberals." A very suspicious lot.)

At Liberal parties, you don't have to pretend to like sherry. Vodka is acceptable. Say you love vodka. Smile, smile, smile. But never flirt. You'll scare hell out of the male Liberal. If you possess a suit of mannish tweeds, that is a really great touch. Wear a turtle neck sweater with it. Be daring. Go to cocktail parties in stretch-pants, and if your legs are ugly so much the better. Look superior. Talk about Sartre.

Imply that you approve of fornication and adultery. Say, "I believe in meaningful relationships between the sexes, for the expansion and growth of the whole personality." Be grim about it. Talk of abortion and demand that it not only be legal but constantly necessary. A lady can talk of these things without fear with a male Liberal, if she speaks boldly and without coquettishness.

Wear boots, even though there is no snow and the weather is warm. Boots are *de rigueur*. They must not be pretty little boots, with tassels and high heels. They must be sturdy. Wear black stockings if you wear a skirt. Wear a Russian short-coat. Gloves are out.

Admire pop art, even if it is composed of old beer bottles, prune pits, wrenches, dog collars, ham bones, and wire. Say it has subtlety and is a condemnation of blatant commercialism. Condemn suburbs, no matter if many of them are pretty, tree-filled, and quiet. Speak of the "decaying cores of our cities." Blame the decay on middle-class "greed."

Make your voice indignantly tremulous when you speak of "the rights of minorities." It isn't of consequence that every man—and woman—jack of us is a "minority" in one way or another. Imply that "society" makes "second-class citizens" of "ethnic groups," and shut your mouth if you feel like saying *you* are a member of an "ethnic group" yourself, as who isn't? Be careful though in speaking of *WASPS* (White Anglo-Saxon Prostestants). You might be talking to one in the guise of a Liberal, and he won't like you to sneer at them, though he will eagerly agree with you that they are dreadful. If you happen to be Catholic or Jewish, his thoughts of you will be silently unkind, and nothing is more deadly than an unkind Liberal. Speak effusively of the late Pope John, who never, poor misused man, said or meant the things Liberals claim he did.

Now, what's holding you back from making the Liberals love and tolerate you?

8

Onomatopoeia

Some time ago a friend of mine, alarmed at my chronic appearance of portending mayhem, gave me some sound advice. "Don't let the Liberal get your blood-pressure up," he said. "Laugh at him. Laughter has killed more farces, frauds, and hypocrites than guns."

Well for the good of my health, I began to try to laugh at the Liberals. I looked at them and laughed some more. But when I listened to them, it really became hilarious. For instance, I discovered the Liberal disease called onomatopoeia. It is his favorite mode of expression, and he encourages it wherever he sets his foot and wherever his eye lights. It is not exactly a disease. It is—well, I will give you samples.

When my husband and I were in New York we received tickets from a young actress whose third (fourth? fifth?) husband was a producer of a successful play on Broadway. I think it was called "The Derelict Hamburger." Well, never mind, we went.

Now, my husband was at home with English, German, French, Spanish, Italian, and all the Slavic languages and some dead ones, too. He also had excellent hearing. During the first act he whispered anxiously, "What did he say?"

"I think," I replied, "they are all speaking Sanskrit."

Marcus gave me a dark look and craned forward, baffled. He said, "I get a word here and there." My hearing wasn't as good as his, and I didn't even get an occasional word. I got up and bought a bag of jelly-beans and sat down and went to sleep all through the play, and even through intermission.

We met the young lady afterwards, and she was all lambent and asked how we had enjoyed the play. I confessed that I had not understood it. The actors and actresses had just stood there and used onomatopoeia. As the young lady had graduated from one of the major chi-chi female colleges, she understandably looked puzzled. (Her vocabulary was still at an elementary school level.) I said, "Let me give you an example. The hero in the first act stood heroically stage front, center, and said, 'Aunsy, duh whoo-whoo.' That was the theme of the whole play, it seems, for I heard it repeated many times. Now, what does 'aunsy, duh whoo-whoo' mean?"

Her face cleared and took on that far, rapturous look of the true Liberal. "Oh!" she exclaimed, and then thought a minute. "Now did he say AUNSY! duh WHOO-whoo, or aunsy DUH whoo-WHOO, or aunsy! duh whoo-WHOO?"

"I think it was the last," I said, utterly fascinated. "What language was he speaking?"

Her glance was a little sharp. You know these brotherly-lovers: Challenge them, and they'll have your lights and livers in a minute, without benefit of their famous "compassion."

"It was method-speaking," she said, and looked at me as if I had just come out of an igloo.

"Explain," said I, undaunted. She tossed her fall of long, uncombed hair and set out to explain. It seems you *never* use ordinary words in the new "communicating." Words take the heart out of what you are trying to communicate. You use the "heart-communication" when you talk to anyone, produce a play, teach a class of children, converse with your loved ones or infants, or just talk. That's the new way, the in way. It's "heart!"

I am constantly having medical disasters and catching my physician off in some hospital on a case, and therefore I usually go to the Emergency Room rather than the doctor's office. So lately I visited another Emergency Room and waited for my haggard physician. There were quite a number of people there in various stages of imminent death, including myself. Near the door sat a young man of about fifteen who had had a spectacular cut on the arm, and it was now swathed in neighbors' handkerchiefs. He wasn't about to die at once, as I was, and sundry other unfortunates. In fact, he looked sprightly and chewed gum at a great rate and stared around with interest at us moribund ones.

Th nurse came into the room and, instead of looking at us basket-cases, her eye lit on the boy near the door, whom I will call Jim. Immediately her eye flashed with loving lightning, and she bent over Jim, and, so help me, the following "conversation" took place:

NURSE (*crooning tenderly*): Een-een-een?

JIM (*looking at his arm*): Un-un-UN.

NURSE: Oh, suh poo-poo-poo! (*She patted his shoulder tenderly.*)

JIM: Awt tuh-tuh mum-mum.

NURSE (*really crooning now*): Oohzi, oohzi, ahahhh.

Jim got up and staggered out with Nanny. The aged gentleman next to me was dying by inches before our eyes, but he said to me, "Foreigners, eh?"

"I don't think so," I said. "They're just 'cummunicating'."

He reared back, glared, and examined me cautiously. "What?" he barked.

"It's the new Liberal jargon," I explained. "Don't you understand it?"

"Me?" he said, outraged. "I'm gonna vote for Wallace!"

The lady on my other side, who was drawing her final breaths—as I was—said, "I think they do it on *purpose*."

I don't. I think they are just too ignorant or too illiterate —to talk "meaningfully" with anyone except each other.

I don't know how I get into these things, but occasionally I accept an invitation to a cocktail party composed mainly of Liberals, although I don't know why I accepted this particular one. I saw at once on entering the house that it was a Liberal establishment. They were serving only sherry and a clam-and-sour-cream dip. I would have run at once but my husband was breathing down my neck and whispering, "Behave!" I figured, What the hell? It was only five o'clock and we could get out of there within ten minutes or so without the sherry and clams.

Now, I was irritated, as I am always irritated at being dragooned under false pretenses into a situation where I am supposed to act civilized in an atmosphere that is totally uncivilized. When the hostess slinked up to me with her loving-loving smile and asked me brightly if she could bring me "something"—I got that one word anyway—I said resoundingly, "Yes! A double bonded bourbon, please." She stared at me. "Oro, ordi, un un?" she asked.

I thought she said ordure, so I said, hopefully, "Ordure?"

"Quit it!" my husband seethed against my nape, and said to the hostess—he was always able to catch on— "Oro, un UN!"

The hostess hurried off, her gold lamé dress rattling, and I said to my husband, "What is 'oro, un un?'"

"Clams!" he shouted, and immediately all conversation stopped, and everyone turned to us. They'd heard an English word and it was verboten, and they were annoyed. My husband, a sensitive chap, could not stand being stared at, and so he colored vividly, gripped my arm and said, "For God's sake, can't you take it for five minutes?"

Well, why should I? Why should I waste my time listening to onomatopoeia? I out-grew that by the time I was eleven months old. The battle lust flared in me. The hostess returned with a small glass of sherry and two damp crackers covered with goo, and I said, "No thanks. This is a fast day."

"Unz?" she asked.

I decided to get into the spirit of things. "Luntz," I said, nodding gamely.

"Awch," she said, nodded wisely, and beetled off somewhere like a knight on the track of the Holy Grail.

"Will you please . . ." my husband said. Then tasted the sherry and made a mouth like a dirty word. He put it down on a chair, where, I am happy to say, a fat lady in a white dress soon sat on it.

I stood and waited, all anticipation to see what my hostess would retrieve somewhere in the house. She soon came back triumphantly—with a glass of water. Now, I have nothing against water—I like to bathe in it. I like to try to swim in it. I think it is very pretty. I even boil lobsters in it. Still, I thought, it might be vodka. I took a sip. It wasn't! The hostess watched, all arch love. "Udd?" she asked.

"Zint," I said, and gave her the glass.

Perfect communication, you see. My husband had a darkly sparkling eye and it was fixed on me now with less than conjugal affection. The lady in the white dress now sat down on his discarded glass, and there was an uproar of onomatopoeia, and we got out of there as fast as oiled eels. "You would!" said my husband, breathing fresh air outside.

"Who put the sherry on the chair?" I asked. "And what —ak-chully—is wrong with communication? I think I made a hit with the hostess. Coming down to it, from the noise I hear back there, someone wants to hit you, too."

"I will never," my husband vowed, "go anywhere with you again."

9

Pioneering in Kentucky

Recently I found myself among a group of "knowledge-able" individuals who were engaged in a discussion on Appalachia and its problems and why the government must conduct a Welfare Program there. "I lived in Appa-lachia," I said, "for nearly five years."

As none of the above had apparently set foot below the Mason-Dixon Line they stared at me blankly. Then one of them said "I heard you never lived anywhere except Buffalo and Rochester, New York, where you were born, and that you've never even been out of the United States or anywhere else, and that your name really was Janet Taylor but you added the name, Caldwell, because of a famous writer, Erskine Caldwell."

"No," I said, "I've never lived in Rochester, and I was born in Prestwich, Manchester, England, and I was bap-tised in the New Bury Methodist Church there when I was six weeks old and christened Janet Miriam Taylor Holland Caldwell. Moreover, I've traveled almost everywhere in this world, and lived not only in Kentucky but in West Virginia, Virginia, and Tennessee."

They didn't believe me, of course. One said, with an air of tender indulgence, "Now, why should you, a famous novelist, ever have lived in Appalachia? A government grant?"

"No, I went with my first husband, a young Virginian. He wanted to get rich quick. He believed—and I practically agree with him now in these days of high taxes— that no one can get rich by merely working for money. The government will take care of that. So, he listened to friends of his in the oil-fields of Kentucky—far back in the mountains—and gave up his job as a construction engineer, and we moved South. We spent five years in the mountains of Kentucky."

They stared. Apparently they had not heard me. "Oh, you were a field worker!"

"No," I said, "I was a nineteen-year-old wife and mother of a year-old child."

"I bet you lived in one of those decayed Southern mansions with Negro servants."

"No," I said, "I lived in a tent. Once or twice, when we were lucky, we lived in an abandoned log cabin, at least two hundred years old."

"Did you say *nineteen*? Why, that's *babyhood!* You were just in school at that age!"

"No, I was a wife and mother, and I was no baby. I was a full-grown mature woman, as all nineteen-year-old women really are, in spite of the 'teen' fad so sedulously cultivated in America."

"Why did your parents let you drop out from school and go into a sort of Peace Corps project financed by the government?" asked another.

"A tent?" cried a lady. "How could you live in a little tent?"

"It was a big square tent, about sixteen-feet square, with

boarded walls half the way up, and screening and canvas curtains to the fly."

The last word made the ladies and gentlemen giggle.

"The fly," I said patiently, "is the cover over the main roof of canvas. It helps insulate against rain and heat and snow, through an air-space. Our big tent was furnished with two beds, cots really, a table and a bench, a commode to hold water and pails, a storage place for food and canned goods—my canned goods—and a kerosene stove for cooking and heating. I also had an orange crate for my dishes, pans, and blankets, and for what linen we possessed.

"We weren't financed by the government, and it was no Peace Corps or Job Corps. I was no high-school dropout. I had finished high school by going at night, from the time I had my first job at the age of fifteen. And I had gone to Appalachia to help get money to finance me through college and to help make us 'rich.'

"We had a mule to ride, when we could catch him, and a cow to milk, when I could catch and milk her, and one hundred chickens for their eggs and meat. I also had to learn to hunt rabbits and squirrels and raccoons, to supplement our miserable larder. I'm an expert at a rifle now —which may come in handy some day," I added, looking at them meaningly, for I was losing my temper. But I went on, daring them not to listen.

"I had to learn to grow vegetables for our table. I had a corn patch, and a patch of lettuce and carrots and radishes, and several hills of potatoes. That was in the mountains, forty miles from the nearest railroad, and five miles from the nearest village. Once a week, I gathered up my baby and my basket and walked those five miles over the mountains, across pastures, and streams, to the little village of Benton to buy staples such as coffee, sugar and salt. I made my own bread, on the kerosene stove. I cured my own bacon and ham in the smokehouse my husband built. We had a couple of sows and a boar, and a number of pigs. I couldn't bear to have them slaughtered—I was a city girl—so I went to Benton for the bacon and ham most of the time. But when slaughtering time came I had to agree to it, and so smoked my own pork."

"And," said a gentleman, "you had pot liquor, too." They all laughed and looked knowing.

"Do you know what pot liquor is?" I asked.

They laughed again. "Oh, moonshine those Kentuckians make."

"No," I said. "Pot liquor is the mingled juice of vegetables and sowbelly fat after you have cooked them for hours in an iron pot. The mountain people don't like raw vegetables. After all, they are a civilized Anglo-Saxon-Celtish people. So they cook their vegetables long and hard, and the water in the bottom of the pot is 'pot liquor' and it's very tasty, too. Good for babies."

"For babies!" shrieked a lady with horror. "Babies should have only pasteurized milk!"

"My baby did very well on the milk of the cow, when I could catch her. She was half wild and I didn't catch her regularly. And I did not pasteurize the milk. And my child drank pot liquor and ate the bacon and ham I smoked, and the vegetables and fruit I canned, and thrived without the benefit of Dr. Spock."

My husband, then twenty-three, had gone to the mountains ahead of me, to prepare things, as he vaguely said. He was a country boy. The country had no terrors for him. So when I was nineteen, I arrived with my baby at Paintsville, Kentucky, the last outpost before the mountains. My husband had arranged for us to be met by a man my own age, with an open wagon filled with straw and drawn by four mules. It was a stormy February day. We rode in wind and snow and hail and rain, unsheltered, for two nights and two days, I, struggling with an umbrella to keep the worst off my baby. When we took shelter for a few hours of sleep it was in a barn or an ancient abandoned log cabin. And around us reared the savage black and white of the lonely mountains, with here and there a little ghost hamlet where I could buy bread and butter and some meat.

The roads were only mud tracks, filled with four and five foot potholes, into which the soggy wagon sank regularly. The four mules struggled to pull us out. Sometimes my "chauffeur" had to get out and dig in the mud to release the wooden wheels. He could neither read nor write. But he was a courteous and manly gentleman, full of kindness and chivalry. He knew that land and the wisdom of it, and he knew I was ignorant of it all. He sang ballads to comfort my crying and very wet baby, and during the worst of the storms he found us shelter. Dear Donnie, I remember him well and with sadness, for only four months later he was killed by a wild mule.

Donnie wrapped old blankets around us. He built fires near the woods and shot rabbits for us, and taught me how to skin and clean and roast them over the fires. He taught me how to make cornbread. Sometimes he'd go into fields and bring back potatoes and carrots and we'd have a fine mountain stew. Donnie gravely said grace before all our meals—out in the open winter storm—and for the first time, really, I knew the grandeur of religion and it was close to me. God was not confined to churches. He was omnipresent. He was beside our rain-soaked open wagon in the wilderness. He stood beside us when we slept. I had known this only academically in my short lifetime.

Donnie, like all traveling mountain folk, had three iron skillets, the first I had ever seen. He cooked delicious meals. He had blue eyes and bright golden hair and a strong and masculine face, full of tenderness. He was all earth and verity. He talked of God as one talks of one's close Father, gently and seriously, and with pride and respect. Nothing irritated him or annoyed him. He moved with confidence and surety. When he shot a squirrel or a rabbit for our meals, he would say, "God made them, and I hate to kill them, but nature is wild and all live on each other. But we shouldn't kill more than we need; that's a sin. And we should always pray that we haven't offended the Father when we shoot one of his little ones. When we plant, we should ask the Father to bless our harvest."

Donnie knew nothing of "socio-economic groups." He did not know he was "underprivileged, disadvantaged or culturally deprived." But he did know the earth, and he knew gallantry and goodness and virtue and the protection of the weak. He had never heard of higher mathematics and "the problems of the adolescent." But he knew when to plant and when to refrain. He knew natural poetry and grandeur. He was serene with the serenity only true men know.

Donnie had a deep, strong, musical voice. He sang old ballads as if they had been written that day. He spoke the mountain speech, which is the speech of old England. He had never heard of Shakespeare, but he had Shakespeare's mordant wit and rhythm of words. His family had lived in the mountains for over three hundred years, and he had been born in the log cabin his ancestors had built. It had only one large room. Donnie had not suffered for lack of modern conveniences. He stood over six feet tall and every foot was muscle and strength and manliness. His mother had never heard of vitamins and a balanced diet. Yet I've not seen, since Donnie, a young man his age so oak-like, so nimble, so utterly masculine, calm and knowing.

He had nine brothers and sisters, and when I saw them later I saw that they were just like Donnie, proud, independent, full of courtesy and kindness. His father had thirty mean acres on the mountains, and he was content. It was enough for Donnie's father when the sun shone and his young cows gave birth and his hogs thrived and his chickens had eggs, and there was a fire on the stone hearth and "the woman" was quilting busily and preserving the fruits of the field and the forests. His children worked in the patches, and what they produced was for the family and what was left over they could sell in the stores. The younger four were going to the school house. "Though," said Donnie's father, "what they need with book-larnin' I don't figure. Makes a man sick."

Donnie's family never had much money, nor did most of the other mountain folk. But they had homemade quilts and bread, their own meat and pork, their stern and loving religion. They enjoyed life. They had pride. They helped their neighbors when help was needed, and were helped in return. When the circuit rider came around four times a year they had revival meetings, and the little log-church was filled to the walls, and everyone sang and rejoiced in the name of the Lord. Twice a year a doctor rode through "from the settlements," but the mountain folk are hardy and rarely were sick. He took his pay in a cured ham or a bag of dried beans or a quarter of a freshly-slaughtered calf, or in flour.

The women of the mountains made their own sheets of brownish cotton, which were later bleached white in the sun. They wove their own thick wool blankets. They needed nothing from the outside world but coffee. Many of them raised sugar beets or cane, and made their own 'lasses. They grew their own wheat and carried it to the miller to be ground. They never saw oranges or lemons or pineapples, but they grew apples and peaches and pears, such as we never see in our supermarkets. They grew grapes. They picked wild huckleberries and blackberries and strawberries, and taught me how to find them and preserve them.

They taught me to hunt, and to raise my own vegetables, and how to make clabber and butter and cornbread. They taught me to sew and to knit. They were kind and affectionate, though I was only an "outlander from the settlements." They had never seen a train or a skyscraper. They had never attended a movie or a theatre or a ballet. They had never walked on pavements. But they were not "deprived." They knew the terror and beauty of storm and the changing seasons; they knew when the river was full and what to do about it to protect their pastures and their fields. They were wise with the earth, and there is no wisdom greater. They would stand at sunset and look at the fire on their dark mountains and they would pray. Then they would turn homeward to their warm kettles and their kerosene lamps, to laughter and song and the sound of their guitars—which they had made, themselves. They returned to love and the warm night and security.

Each Saturday night, in Benton, the mountain folk would stream down to the village to dance their ancient square dances in what they called "the barn," which served as a church the next day. The women would bring baskets of food and the men would bring their "white mule." The children were always there, also, to midnight. I have never seen such real gaiety as I saw then, with the women's calico skirts flying, and the banjos and the guitars singing, and the heavy boots thudding on the plank floors. The faces were bright with simple joy and pride and affection. The evil cities were far away, with their crime and hatred and lust and envy and murder and lies. The Sheriff lived in Benton and had a big farm. He also had a one-cell jail which was rarely occupied.

Man, woman and child, they knew the Constitution and the Bill of Rights for which their ancestors had fought and bled and died, and God help anyone who infringed on them! They lived the law and their religion, and they worked pridefully and thriftily. And they'd toil up the mountainside where we lived in our big tent and tell my husband, "We got worryin' bout that big gal of yourn, and the little gal, and so my woman baked this bread and here's a ham for you."

There were "outlanders" all through the region, with their poisonous cigarettes, city men from Louisville and Richmond and all over, drilling for oil. The mountain folk were uneasy. But they gave permission for drilling on their land. When the money rolled in—sometimes over a thousand dollars a week—the mountain folk were indifferent. The money piled up in the "settlement" banks, and stayed there, untouched. Money was unimportant to the men of the land, who had their herds and their fields, and their snug cabins and their religion.

Life and birth and death were accepted with no cries, no complaints. It was all a part of living, and who quarrelled with God and the earth?

I won't say it was a glorious life for me, out there on the naked mountains in a fragile tent, and all alone twelve hours of the day with a toddler. I won't say I enjoyed going far down the mountainside with my pails to the artesian well for water, and then climbing up again with the sloshing buckets. It wasn't delightful for me, loaded down with a baby and carrying a basket, to dodge roaring bulls and wild horses in the pasture over which I had to walk "down to Benton" for necessities. Riding a mule—when we could catch him—or an ox—when we could catch him—isn't the most comfortable way to travel. But I did learn something of invaluable worth.

I learned how to build a cabin and to roof it. I learned how to plow the ground and to plant. I learned how to shoot for meat. I learned how to make all our clothing and what herbs to gather to make medicine. I learned to weave wool rugs and blankets. I knew the berries which were poisonous and those which I could can. In short, I knew how to survive in the wilderness, even to delivering a baby, even to grinding grain for bread. I knew how to make a dwelling place immune to weather, and how to build fires and bleach cotton. I still know, and it is all a cherished part of my knowledge.

After we had lived two years in Benton, we moved to Bowling Green. My husband never discovered the oil for which he was drilling in Appalachia. He worked for a Liberal who lived grandly, and who promised wonders for the young exploited who labored for him in his fields. He

would "invest" their wages, he said, in "my growing oil
empire. Nothing too good for my boys." Finally he owed
my husband a thousand dollars, and thousands more to
other innocents working for him. So he promptly filed for
bankruptcy, claiming no assets. He had everything in his
wife's name.

So, we found ourselves with no money at all except fifty
dollars I had made, myself, as a public stenographer. I
walked from the farmhouse, where we boarded, six miles
into town, worked all day, then walked the six miles back.
I had had this job for only six months, and with constant
work I could average about eighteen dollars a week which
paid our board and left a little over for savings. I was
twenty-two. I had a four-year-old daughter. There was
no future for us in Bowling Green. But in my home city,
in the North, I could get a regular job as a secretary and
make, I hoped, twice as much. There wasn't enough
money for the three of us to travel on, so I left my husband in Kentucky trying to find enough work to raise his
fare, and took my child home.

It was no fun traveling two nights and one day in a
gritty coach with a little girl. I had my trunk with me,
something like a foot-locker of small dimensions, and in
it I had all my worldly goods, including clothing for myself and my child for all seasons, fifty or so books, two old
blankets, and two iron skillets.

The fare had been twenty-nine dollars, and then there
was the expense of food on the train and some cough-
mixture for my child, who had developed a bad cold on
the journey and was quite sick. I arrived in Buffalo in a
particularly savage February blizzard—and with no place
to go and with only about fifteen dollars in my purse. It
was 6:30 A.M., black and below zero. We emerged into
the station and I spent fifty cents for our breakfast. Then
I bought a newspaper and sat down to study the ads. First
of all, I had to find a place to live.

My hopes were high, and so were my spirits, and so I

bought my child a sucker to keep her quiet on the bench in the waiting-room of the station while I studied the morning newspaper. It never occurred to me that I was in a desperate plight. Therefore, I was in no such plight. I was soon enlightened, and I have never forgotten the shame, the embarrassment, and the mysterious if momentary terror and loathing.

A middle-aged gaunt woman suddenly sat down next to me, curiously smelling of camphor and an unwashed body and hair that needed laundering. She was dressed in thick, dark-brown wool and a drab hat. My little girl took the sucker out of her mouth and, with the instinct of childhood, moved closer to me for protection. I stared at the woman and shifted a little away from her, but she followed me, and, to my outrage, began to stroke my arm.

"In trouble, dear?" she murmured.

I had been taught by my mother never to speak to strangers. Still I was polite, so I told the woman as briefly as possible that I was searching the newspaper for a boarding house for me and my child, and a possible job. She cocked her head as she listened. Her eyes moistened. She kept stroking my arm, and now her hand began to linger on my neck which she kept gently mauling and pinching. It gave me the shudders. Then abruptly she took my purse off my lap and opened it. I snatched at it, sure I had encountered a thief, but she was only counting my money. "Fifteen dollars," she mused, "and no home, nowhere to go. Poor children." She returned my purse, and returned to fondling my neck. Now I was frightened, and she saw it.

"Oh, I represent the County Welfare," she reassured me. "Tell me, dear, are you married?" When I angrily told her that I was indeed married, she looked disappointed. "Take your hand off my neck," I told her. She gave me a final loving pinch, and withdrew her hand. "Such a pretty girl, too," she murmured. "Under your circumstances, dear," she said, "would you be willing to put your child up for adoption? We have so many calls . . ."

My mouth fell open in amazement. "What do you mean, my circumstances?" I demanded.

"Your poverty, dear, your terrible poverty."

"I'm not poor!" I shouted. Had she accused me of the grossest immorality I could not have felt more disgraced, more ashamed, more degraded.

"But fifteen dollars, and no place to go!"

"Get out of here!" I cried, trying to keep from bursting into horrified tears.

"But, I want to help," she cooed. "We have shelters. We will place your child in a home, and give you counselling, and a warm place to sleep. While you consider putting up your child for adoption—such a pretty little baby, too. . . ."

Someone halted before me, and I looked up to see a Salvation Army lady standing beside me, a woman with a rosy maternal face and the kindest eyes. (I saw the kindness later, for at that time she was staring at the Welfare lady coldly and sternly.) Then she said to me, "Is there anything the matter, child?"

The bonnet and the cloak and the air of cleanliness and kindness and the blue sweet eyes were reprieve and haven to me. I began to talk, but the Welfare lady interrupted and said, "Captain, I don't think this is one of your cases, so please don't interfere. I am trying to persuade this girl to give up her child and accept Welfare . . ."

The Captain ignored her. "I don't want to be impolite," she said to me, "but perhaps I can give you advice, at least." She sat down on my other side and smiled at me and then in a motherly fashion she wiped my baby's nose. Then she said to the Welfare lady, "Please leave us."

The creature stood up. "I am going to call the police and have this girl arrested as a vagrant, for her own good!" she said. "She has no home, no means of support, no money to speak of, and no place to go!"

"Yes, she has," said the Salvation Army Captain. "She has us, and I'm in charge here. Run along," her face suddenly severe. "If you don't leave, Miss, I'll have a few words with the police, myself, and I don't think you'll like what I have to say."

The woman left, to my overwhelming relief. The Captain settled beside me, and she smelled of soap and freshness and that cleanliness of heart and soul which has its own special fragrance.

"Well," she said briskly, "the first thing is to find some nice boarding house where you can stay until you get a job." She brought out a black notebook from her big bag and went through it. "Just the people!" she said. "Mr. H—— is sixty-five and he has quite a good job, selling shoes, but his wife is an invalid. A very refined lady. They have an unmarried daughter, about my age, who cares for her mother. They do need extra money, and they are very proud. They have a nice bedroom for rent, for two, and three meals a day. Fifteen dollars a week."

I considered. I had nothing to sell that would bring me a couple of dollars. I told the Captain that I couldn't pay board in advance, until I had a job, for I needed the fifteen dollars I had. She nodded. "Oh, I'm sure it can all be arranged. Let me make a telephone call or two."

She was back in minutes, beaming. "It's all right," she said, "I talked with Miss H——, the daughter, and she accepts my recommendation. She and her parents are part of our Army. They are waiting for you and your child. Now, just give me your baggage ticket, and we'll be on our way."

We were, in five minutes, followed by my little trunk. When we reached the outside it was just getting light and the blizzard was blinding. The Welfare lady was talking to two policemen, and as we emerged from the station the three of them swung to me. "There are the waifs!" she cried.

The policemen came towards us. I was overcome with

terror and a feeling of nightmare. I wanted to lift my
child and run. But the Captain took my arm firmly. She
smiled at the policemen. "No," she said, "these are not
waifs. Everything is arranged, gentlemen." She looked up
at them with her clear blue eyes, and they touched their
caps.

"Private charity!" spat the Welfare woman.

"Not charity," said the Captain. "Just temporary assist-
ance."

"This girl and her child aren't vagrants then?" asked
one of the policemen.

"Of course not! She just needed a boarding house for
herself and her child, and there's plenty of work in her
line—secretarial. I helped her find the boarding house,
and everything's fine, officer."

The Captain nodded and smiled and led me to the curb
to a taxi. "I can't afford it," I said. I was still trembling.
I clutched my child to my side.

"Oh, but you have a trunk. Just return the fare, when
you have a job."

So we rode in style through the howling blizzard to my
new home. It was a big old wooden house, warm and
clean, and the mother and the daughter greeted us as
though we were dearly-beloved young relatives returning
from a long journey. They were poor. I know now how
dreadfully poor they were. But they were proud and filled
with the true sense of brotherhood; respect for others'
privacy and pride and self-respect. I was no vagrant to
them, no poor soul who needed help. I was a husky
young woman, a wife and a mother, in temporary difficulties which she could solve herself.

"You need more than fifteen dollars a week," said
the Captain, helping me to unpack what little I had in the
warm room with its double bed. "You need fifteen for
board for you and Mary, and then there's carfare and
lunches for yourself, and money for clothing, a little later.
So, you need about twenty-five dollars a week. Report

to Mr. Lester Schweitzer tomorrow morning. He is in the insurance and real-estate business; not very successful, I'm afraid, but he's willing to pay twenty-five dollars for a good secretary. There's a depression on, you know, and I just don't understand what all the newspapers are roaring about—saying we are so prosperous and everyone has so much money."

That was in 1923. There certainly was prosperity, but it was a gangster prosperity, a gunmoll prosperity, a thieves' prosperity. I found out later that twenty-five dollars a week was the average income of individuals and families—that is, for the honest and hard-working. But it was indeed the Roaring Twenties for the criminal of all classes and occupations, the suspect businessmen, the call girls, the stock salesmen and such.

I reported to Mr. Schweitzer the next morning. Mr. Schweitzer had a tiny dank office with two desks in it, one window, and a smell of dust. It was obvious to me that things were not booming. He told me that he averaged about fifty dollars a week, and sometimes when he was lucky, seventy-five. But he needed a secretary, and the Captain had told him I needed twenty-five dollars a week, and we were in business.

Secure in my job, and with my child well cared for by the H—— family, I was happy and busy. A few months later Mr. Schweitzer called my attention to state examinations for court reporter, and he let me take his typewriter to the place of the examinations, and I passed. Eighteen hundred dollars a year! Riches! Magnificent! Mr. Schweitzer and I were in tears when we parted.

"Trust in God, child," he said, holding my hand. "Work hard. Owe no man. Accept nothing you can't repay. Keep your head high. And you'll succeed." I had often discussed my ambitions to be a novelist with him.

He gave me a five-dollar gold piece, which I tried to refuse. But he wanted me to have it, "as a talisman." I never saw him again. He died three months later.

Within a few months I could send my husband money
for his train fare. I had started a bank account. I had some
new clothes for myself and the child. Moreover, Mr.
Schweitzer had informed me what to do about the robber
who had gone into bankruptcy in Bowling Green, and so
deprived my husband of his thousand dollars. I found a
lawyer who went to work on the case. He collected nine
hundred dollars for us, and took one hundred for his
fee. We were millionaires! I passed the college board
entrance exams and started night college. And paid for
every penny of it, myself.

Though it was the Roaring Twenties then and a Big Ball
—for a few—my husband was not able to find steady work
in his line. When he did, the pay was miserable, though
again we had no complaint. Then our child became seriously ill. The doctor we called ordered her to the hospital,
into a private room with nurses around the clock. She
was there for over two months, and the costs were high.
Our savings vanished. I was the only one working. Eventually, we were nearly a thousand dollars in debt to the
hospital and the doctor.

I went to the Reverend Mother in charge of the Sisters'
Hospital. I told her frankly of our position. "I can't pay
you all, right away," I said. "But I have a good job, one-
hundred-fifty a month, and will pay it off in stages." I
went to the doctor and told him the same thing. It took me
three years to pay it off, and I never congratulated myself.
I was only doing my duty. No one was responsible for my
predicament; it was all my own. To have offered charity
and free medical and hospital care would have been received, by me, as the supreme insult. To help pay the
debt off sooner, I took a job in a florist's shop on Sundays.

We stayed with the H——s for several years, working
and saving. I was able to contribute to the Salvation Army,
that blessed organization of good and holy people, who
promoted pride and self-respect among those they helped
and who believed, and still believe, in the power of the

individual to solve his own problems, with the help of God.

"Owe no man," old Mr. Schweitzer had told me. Once he added "He who eats the bread of charity has bartered away his own soul, for only an animal accepts what he has not earned." But alas, the Schweitzers are nearly a lost breed in America now, where millions of the inferior are not only urged to take charity but are encouraged to do so, to the loss of their stature as men.

"Poverty is a state of mind." But it is not the state of the soul that refuses to consider itself poor, and has the fortitude to work for what it eats and what it drinks. The really poor are those without ambition and pride and determination. We can't let them starve. However, they should be made to understand that charity is only temporary—and meager—and that it is up to them to get off their knees and walk as men. At least, that is what charity should tell them, and charity is evil if it does not, whether it is private or public.

I "owe not any man," not money, not education, not opportunity. I was a young girl, and I understood even from earlier childhood that we must stand alone—or lose our souls. It is a joy to people of my generation to know that we fought the world with the help of God, and were triumphant. How dare we deny this joy to our grandchildren? The rules whereby we lived are still the rules of life. Those who abrogate them are dooming our country. Cowardly soft nations invite the attentions of the barbarian—and the barbarian is looking over the oceans at us now and estimating how weak we are, how dependent, how feeble of heart and courage. They, at least, know how to work and how to live austerely, and they depend only on themselves. The history of Rome will be our history—unless we call our children to strength, self-denial, and responsibility again.

10

What Happened to American Men?

This is a tough world and a violent one and always was and always will be.

But I do believe in love. (Not "luv" you will notice.) I have been in love more times than I can remember, and invariably at first sight, and wildly and devotedly. Whether or not this was always requited slips my mind, but I sure was in love early and always from the age of eight on. I dearly love masculine persuasion, though now my head is bloody if unbowed, and there is a hint or two of gray hairs. I loved one relative—not in my immediate family —and I love my children. And I love my God and my country above all else.

Well, that is love, not "luv."

When God suggested, "Love thy neighbor as thyself," I hope I am not being irreverent for suspecting that this was an example of Divine Humor. I believe that the Source of so much laughter and innocent gaiety, and the frolicking of blameless animals in dewy fields, and the multitude of endless paradoxes in the world, must be deeply fond of a good joke. That admonition to "love thy neighbor" is very subtle and humorous, for what *intelligent* man—aware of himself, his sins and his limitations, and his miserable status in life, his secret nastinesses and unspeakable private little crimes, and his tendency to malice—can *"love"* himself?" It takes an egotistic clod, with a poverty of experience, to look with either kindness or affection on his own person. If one is to credit the headshrinkers and the philosophers and theologians of the past, the source of much human misery is a deep and hidden self-loathing and rejection, though frankly I consider such emotions salutary and suspect they keep a man in a proper frame of mind and with a sense of proportion. That's why I appreciate the Lord's wit and careful language when He suggested, "Love thy neighbor as thyself." If there is any good in this world it comes not only from a candid self-appraisal and even self-rejection, but from a rejection of those traits in our brothers which make us all a little less than appetizing.

I confess that I have interpreted that particular commandment of loving your neighbor as yourself as meaning that you should have respect for your neighbor's rights, and should show him kindness and sympathy or at least tolerance, if he is half-way decent. But if he is an unregenerate s.o.b. and a fool or a criminal or a mendicant, or is triumphantly proud of his stupidity and will not learn from experience or from the wisdom of the ages, then as the Koran advises, avoid him always. Love is a two-way street, and the unlovable should curb his disgusting traits and pull up his socks and be a man if he wants the respect of his fellows.

In these perilous days, alas, the Liberals are talking incessantly of "luv." You must "luv" and you must be "warm" even if your neighbor turns your stomach and you know that he ought to be in jail, or his personal habits revolt you. This, of course, is pure sanity. For myself, I am

usually in control of my less lovable traits, for I know
public, or even private mayhem is frowned upon in
civilized society. Then, too, the other guy may be able to
hit harder.

There was a time even in my remembrance when
American men were manly, heads of their houses, and
respected by their wives and children. They were rugged
and hard-nosed and not swamped in a soft pink jello.
A thief was a thief to them, and not a "disadvantaged,
underprivileged, culturally deprived" weakling. I've seen
men beat up other men who attempted to snatch a
woman's purse on the public streets, or who kicked a dog
or punched a child. To be sure, American men demanded
to be respected, and not "loved" in those nostalgically
remembered days. They'd have laughed in your face if you
had asked: "But don't you Love?" They'd have said,
"Yes, I love my God and my country, and my family. I
respect my neighbor's humanity and won't infringe on his
rights—so long as he doesn't infringe on mine. But 'love'
him? Are you crazy?"

Americans in those days were adult, and men were
masculine, women were feminine, and there was no blurring of the sexes. A man's word was law in his home, no
matter how shrewish his wife, and God help the kid who
questioned the father's edict. Of course, in those benighted
eras of American masculinity, kids didn't become "juvenile
delinquents," nor did they smoke marijuana or imbibe
L.S.D., nor were their pockets stuffed with money, nor
did they ride around in cars. The car was Papa's property,
used by Mama only on sufferance. And Papa held the
purse strings, so there was no extravagance, no wild buying of worthless tinsel and gadgets and widgets. Best of
all, there were no pants, figuratively or literally, on ladies'
legs.

In short, women were happier then, and so were the
kids. Papa wasn't expected to change Baby's diapers nor
get his bottle in the middle of the night, nor did he wipe

the dishes, or run a vacuum cleaner, or "be a pal to the children." Papa had nights out with the Boys, and if he came home a little beery, and late, Mama knew enough to keep her mouth shut. If a man in those days had said, "I am taking a poorer job with shorter hours so I can spend more time with The Children," his peers would have thought he was out of his mind.

A popular woman's magazine lately held a poll among its readers, asking how they designated their husbands in their minds and in their "projects." Not one single lady replied that her husband was authority, friend, companion. Indeed not. All of them designated their husbands as "homeowner," "children's friend," "father" or—God help us—"helper." In brief, Papa was a sort of surrogate Mama, existing solely to feed Mama's offspring and provide shelter for them. I detected an unconscious contempt in their replies.

Now, what has caused American men to abdicate their position as men, as citizens, as protectors of the weak, as watchers of Washington, as strong-armed and masculine creatures who were a delight to the eyes, the hearts and the arms of their women-folk? And a pride to their children? Is it, as some claim, because women teachers are permitted to teach boys, and that women have entirely too much influence in this country? I don't know. But a man isn't deprived of his manhood, as in some Oriental countries, except by his consent.

In some fashion, men in America have been deprived of their manhood; and whether they permitted their women to do that is a moot question. If they did, why did they permit it? Why have they left the larger business of watching Washington and studing the national budget, and taking a passionate interest in politics and the state of the beer in their saloon, and making a good living, for the womanish business of cosseting kids and being a good, loving dad and a sort of housemaid?

Again, who unmanned our men? Who has made so

many millions of them sickly homosexuals and weaklings dependent on government hand-outs, and shameless mendicants at the public troughs? Who has encouraged them to cry for more Welfare schemes and more schools and more recreation for the children? Who has turned them from manly lovers of their wives to unmanly lovers of their fellow men? Who has taken the pants off our men and put skirts and aprons on them? And who has made of our women imitation men with coarse husky voices, wide strides, arrogance, and muscles?

Look at your TV some night, at "family situation comedies" for verification of the frightful state of men and their unfortunate women. The husband is usually depicted as a stupid halfwit, a buffoon, an ignoramus needing the guidance of wise, witty and waspish Mama; a fool to his own children, and a clown falling over his own feet. His children are depicted as clever, indulgent towards Daddy's stupidity, aides to Mama, and family counselors. Are American men really like this? Or is there a nefarious scheme afoot to make them so?

My Liberal pals always smile when I pose this question to them and they say, "Do you really believe the Communists are responsible for what you call unmanning of American men?" No, I answer, I believe you are. I tell them, "You are without real heart and spirit, enviers of real men—in spite of your empty pipe and your tweeds. If you had manhood, you wouldn't be asking for more bounty from the pockets of your neighbors, via taxes, and more benefits and more 'security.' In order to make your beggar's dream come true it is necessary for you to remove the manhood from other men, and it seems you are succeeding."

Somehow, when I tell them that, they don't "love" me any longer; but they never deny the accusation, either. For they know only too well that it is they who have "encouraged"—one of their more loathsome and presently popular words—women to demand dominance in America and men to submit to that dominance. They have "encouraged" young people to despise their fathers and feel superior to the man who feeds their bottomless stomachs and clothes them. They have made fools of our fathers, our brothers, our husbands, our sons. If it is true, as is alleged, that more and more women are becoming alcoholics in their sanitized suburbs, it is because they have lost—in the deeper meaning of the word—their husbands. They have lost their authority, their lovers, their companions, their friends. They have lost what God gave them, and may God help them.

When men are unmanned, spiritually if not physically, then a country becomes depraved, weak, degenerate, feeble of spirit, dependent, guideless, sick. Such a country can never resist authoritarian despots, tyrannies, the men on horseback, Communism.

The men who once gloried in their race and their country, now smirk at the sight of their flag, duck their heads in embarrassment when religion is mentioned and run from the sight of the attacked helpless; they are terrified of becoming involved. They leave government in the hands of despicable politicians. What resistance will such wretches put up against internal and external Communism?

Europeans laugh at this desire of American men "to be loved," and I am sure all of us have heard that broad and knowing laughter. "Why are Americans such fanatics about needing to be 'loved'?" they have asked, in articles and before audiences. "Is it a sign of weakness?" Indeed it is.

I have watched sessions at the UN on television, and it is not very pleasant to see the covert smiles of contempt when some American spokesman meekly expresses his soft opinion. And why should they not smile? The hand in the velvet glove is not iron. The voice is not the voice of a man. The will to strike in the name of freedom has been drugged by sentimentality. The desire for justice has been polluted by false compassion. America has become the clown of the world because she has permitted the Liberal to deprive her of her sword, and the will to use it.

Our Presidents are always talking about our image abroad. I have news for them. Our "image" is a surrogate Mama, in an apron, with a baby's bottle in his hand. Surrogate Mama to a laughing and contemptuous world! Bottle-feeder to ravenous "infants" to proclaim themselves heads of some obscure state in some backyard continent!

That is our image abroad. Does it make a nice picture to you? Then do something about it. Start in your own house, and then with your own local government. Unseat your emasculators in Washington. Drive them from your schools and your courts. Proclaim to the world again—and again—that you will stand no more nonsense, and that our flag is to be honored wherever it flies over any embassy; that you have power and are quite willing to use it, in the name of freedom and justice, tempered only slightly by masculine mercy.

Then, perhaps, America will be honorably feared and respected, and peace might really come to a mad and disordered world. The center that "cannot hold" might tighten and become iron and invincible, and Doomsday thus averted.

11

Women's Lib

The Left, alas, is now running yet *another* "Liberation Movement," this one championing females who believe that the male sex has somehow done the ladies wrong. The members of this Front say they want all the spoils the boys appear to be getting out of life. They're quite mad, of course. What these "girls" are about to do is to ruin the biggest Con Game, and the most ancient, which one section of humanity has ever imposed on another, since Eve invented it.

I'm just jealous, myself, having been deprived by circumstances from getting into that Big Con Game . . . alas, alas, alas. But I've stood on the sidelines and seethed with envy, and now I hope—I say with a grin over clenched teeth—that the Liberation "girls" will get exactly what they want. It is all they deserve.

I am convinced that the Liberationist females, judging from their photographs at least, and on some personal observation, are so unattractive mentally, physically, and in personality, that they are envious because they can't even *qualify* for the Big Con Game, and so don't want other women to wallow in it with sweet and secret smiles. As for myself, I am only wistful, and plenty happy that my two beautiful daughters are in on the Game and enjoying every minute of it, and wouldn't even dream of Female Liberation. I brought them up to appreciate their blessings—and to shut their mouths around their husbands, for fear the boys would catch on *and demand liberation for themselves*. Which is exactly the calamity these rampant females in the "Liberation Movement" are going to precipitate. God help the contented women who will be their victims!

The Liberation Ladies would have just loved my Mama, who was very advanced and ultra-modern, even more than most women of today. Mama believed in rearing girls exactly as boys were reared, and no nonsense about the weaker sex and the softer yearnings in a girl's heart. Mama believed that what a boy could, and should, do a girl could and should do also; and if a girl had softer muscles and more tender feelings, well that was tough.

So, I was reared just as my brother was reared—except that Little Brother was somewhat smarter than I was and ran his own Con Game against Mama, and succeeded to an enviable extent.

From early childhood I hauled heavy scuttles of coal in from the coal shed, in England, for my parents' fires. The housemaid refused to do it. "It's a man's job," she would say, but Papa, having a dominant wife, lay down on the job. Mama, who had a convenient memory, forgot that what a man can do a woman can, too, and did not haul the coals. She remembered *that* only when it came to me. So I did the hauling, and nearly pulled my arms from the sockets in the rain and the snow and the harsh winds of a British winter.

I did notice that the young daughters of our neighbors did not stoke the fireplaces and drag scuttles, nor clean out the fireplaces in the cold grey dawns. The fathers and the boys of the family did this, while the Mamas and the daughters stayed snuggled-up in bed. My first resentment began, but being a discreet child and knowing the weight of Mama's hand I said nothing. Ah, Mama was a *real* Liberation Movement in herself!

And when we came to America, guess who did most of the stoking of the huge furnace and the carrying out of ashes. Right. I did. "There's nothing wrong with you," Mama would say, roughly, when I felt that I would collapse. "What a boy your age can do you can do, too. Girls are just as strong as boys. You're not going to pamper yourself as long as I am around here!"

Then, there were the enormous snows, often reaching four feet, almost as high as I was. I had to take the weighty coal shovel and get rid of the snow, all by myself. "No coddling here, just because you are a girl," said Mama. See how she echoes the Liberation Ladies of today? My ears would ring and my arms scream with exertion, and my heart would pound in my throat. Neighbors would notice, with outrage, but when one of them complained gently to Mama she would say sturdily, "What a boy can do a girl can do! No cosseting in our house!"

When I was fifteen and an adult, Mama decided that I was quite old enough to go to work—at the first work I could obtain. I was an Adult and should have a job. So, I was pulled out of school and sent job-hunting, and I found heavy laboring work in a factory, six days a week, twelve hours a day. "Why shouldn't a woman do the same work a man does?" the Liberation Ladies of today ask. Girls, I wish to God you had had a Mama like mine! You'd be silent these days, instead of noisy and stupid. I stood on my feet for those twelve hours a day, at a machine, bending and stooping and hauling, in danger from wheels and lathes and whatever. I worked like a man all right.

It was around this time that I first noticed that Boys

were not all as objectionable as Little Brother, and that
some Boys did not resemble Papa in the least. The first
feminine instincts began to stir in my fifteen-year-old
heart. The Boys were in the factory, and sometimes
when they saw me panting too heavily they would force
me to sit down for a few minutes and take my place, in
mercy, at the monstrous machine. And it was about that
time that I began to dream of someday marrying a kind
and considerate husband, one who would cherish me and
know me for a female and not a Liberated Woman, and
take care of me and love and pamper me and hold me
precious as a queen, and buy a pleasant house for me
where I'd have nothing to do but housework and taking
care of children—children quite unlike Little Brother—
and shop and cook. I would no longer have to be anxious
about carfare and worry if my allowance would cover
lunch, and I'd have pretty clothes and be protected all my
life—with no effort on my part. (Alas, alas, alas!)

After work, the snow-shoveling and the carrying of
ashes was still my job, and to this had been added outside
window-washing, gutter-cleaning, grass-cutting and culti-
vating, and shingle-repairing. Papa, prodded by Mama,
was quite an overseer. He would stand, smoking his pipe,
while I teetered on a long ladder and pounded shingles
and nails into the roof, and he directed my efforts. Papa,
too, would have loved the modern Liberation Movement
for Women. Frankly, I think he and Mama invented it.

When I infrequently complained, pleading exhaustion,
Mama would toss her head with a triumphant warning
smile, and say, "What a man can do a woman can do!
There's no difference. Sex has nothing to do with it!"
Just once, seeing Papa hanging up the laundry, I sar-
castically remarked, "And what a woman can do a man
can do, too." This earned me a clout from Mama.

My Aunt Pollie and my Uncle Willie lived not far from
us. Aunt Pollie was not a feminist. She was a lovely gracious lady with long blonde hair and big blue eyes and a

dainty charming manner. She had a Mama, too, but fortunately a Victorian Mama who believed that a woman's place was in her house, and she a queen in her house, and that gentlemen were born for the cherishing, guarding, loving, and pampering of ladies. (Ah, me!)

To Aunt Pollie, Ladies were Ladies. Gentlemen earned mysterious livings "at business," and it was none of the Ladies' affair, except when it came to wills. Girl-children were brought up in the graceful womanly arts of cooking, house-managing, children-rearing, sewing, embroidering —and civilized leisure. It was a woman's place to be an ornament and a comforting presence in her home, adored alike by husband and children, and never was she to be exposed to the harsh elements of competition and outside work, and it was incredible that she should ever be expected to be a "partner" to her husband. She was above such nonsense. She was her husband's queen, presiding beautifully over the table he provided and over the silver-covered dishes, the contents of which she had toothsomely prepared herself. As for holding a job and "helping out," Aunt Pollie would have raised a gilt eyebrow in incredulous amusement. Such things were "below" a woman's existence.

Aunt Pollie, clothed exquisitely and smelling delightfully of perfume, would go with her redoubtable Mama to twice-weekly matinees, then come home to prepare fragrant tea and bake luscious scones to be eaten with homemade strawberry jam. Though she had no modern washing machine and used flat irons and hung out her laundry and had no vacuum cleaner and other "aids," she managed to look serene and rested at all times, and had many hours of leisure every day.

Aunt Pollie, the Queen, a gentle and lovely wife, a "dependent" wife with no ambitions to do a man's work in the world, would have been despised by feminists and the Liberation Ladies. But Aunt Pollie was truly a woman, and not a grotesque neuter full of envy of the male sex—

who have always had it much harder than women, with much less physical stamina, and have been conned by women for endless centuries to make life soft for them.

Unlike our brawling household, Aunt Pollie's house was a place of sweet quiet refuge for a tired girl like myself. Even at the cost of having to go with Uncle Willie to his grim Scots Presbyterian Church on Sunday evenings, I would visit Aunt Pollie for the soothing joy of being in a real home, among soft voices and gentle music, among fragrances and graciousness, and topping it off a real British Tea, produced apparently without effort. And I observed that Uncle Willie was masculinely deferential to Auntie's femininity, elaborately courteous to her, and overwhelmingly loving, while she cosseted him daintily in her female fashion.

Aunt Pollie was a discreet Scots-woman, so she did not criticize my parents and the back-breaking labor she knew I was doing all the long hours of the week. But once she said to me, seriously, in her beautifully modulated voice, "Janet, the only way out for you is more education and then . . . and then breaking away."

It was to Aunt Pollie that I took my literary efforts—written long after midnight and before my rising at six A.M. She would read them closely and carefully, then gaze at me with her tender thoughtful eyes, and repeat my need for more education. So, I went to night high school five nights a week. And believe me, kiddies, at fifteen—a "child," to use modern parlance—I had very little time to sleep or eat after that! There were no adolescent "difficulties" or "traumas," either, no "turmoils," no "rebellions." Life had become a stern business of surviving each day and working and living for the future. The rage still lives in me that despite the financial comforts of my family I was expected to do a boy's and man's work, and "no nonsense about you being a girl, either." All I wanted to be was a girl, and then a cherished woman! Alas.

While I worked and studied, my dream of being the

Cherished Woman—like Aunt Pollie—grew stronger in
me. But all the hard work I had had to do since I was a
child, and the living I had had to earn since I was fifteen,
and all the exhortations I had had to listen to at "home,"
gave me too much independence of manner, too much self-
assurance, too much of an appearance of confidence. This
definitely put off men who wanted a Queen for their
houses, a soft and yielding gentle sweet creature like Aunt
Pollie, a charming hostess pliant and soothing and full of
musical laughter and kind wit. For such a woman men
were ready to work their poor hearts out, considering
themselves blessed. But a girl like myself, who knew hard
labor, and knew how to earn a buck, and had a sharp and
independent voice and manner, was not attractive to
them. They did not want a "partner," and a fellow wage-
earner. They did not believe that a "woman can do anything a man can do." They were right, of course.

So, I did not attract the manly men I secretly adored,
the masculine strong men, the cherishers of women, the
protectors of women, the admirers of women, the men
who believed it was their duty to provide for wives and
children, the men who built nice houses for their women,
who guided them against the evil brutalities of living. I
attracted the weak sisters among the men, who subconsciously recognized that here was a girl who would earn a
living for them, take care of them, protect them, and be
the man of the house, while they indulged their "sickly"
physiques and their "ailments" and their delicate psyches.
They clung to me, the creeps, begging for instant marriage
—with an eye on my pay check—while the men I yearned
for married helpless little creatures who knew nothing of
"business" except it provided them, via men, with the luxuries and comforts of life, and the protection. But, of
course, they had not had my own dolorous life, and had
not had the parents I had.

At eighteen I fell desperately in love with a true man, a
man of strength and masculine vitality and courage. He

was attracted to me, too. But then one night he said to me,
"Janet, you aren't the gentle little woman my mother was.
My father worshipped her, and no wonder. You are too
strong, yourself, and too independent for me. There'd be
conflict in the house. You wouldn't be satisfied just to be
taken care of; you'd want to do something on your own,
and be a 'partner' to me. It's just no use."

I was struck dumb at this horrifying statement. I wasn't
very articulate then. He gently picked up my hands and
shook his head at the old callouses, and as gently put them
down. I wanted to cry out at him, "But I *want* to be like
your mother! I *want* you to take care of me and deliver me
from my hateful daily job! I *want* you to cherish me! I
want only to be your wife and have your children and
keep your house! I don't *want* a career or anything else. I
just want you."

But I couldn't say it. I had no words. My rearing si-
lenced me. And so I never saw him again. But I saw the
creeps, all right! They hung on me like leeches. Charity
prevents me from elaborating on the matter. After all, a
girl has to marry *someone,* doesn't she, when her yearning
for love and protection overcomes her. And believe me,
unless she is a dyke or a Liberated Commie, that yearning
is natural and heart-breaking.

I am too old now to have dreams, or to hope for them. It
was only very recently, however, that I had to abandon
the old desperate yearning to be a wife only, loved and
cherished and protected, guarded by the serene walls of
her house and her devoted husband, her days full of calm
and sunlight and leisure, with no infernal damned career
to follow, with no one dependent on her earnings for
sustenance. And I look on the ladies who have never been
forced to work as I have been forced, the ladies who are
adored by their husbands and provided for by their husbands, who garden placidly and drive out for lunches, and
shop, and know nary a moment of financial anxiety and
never the pressure of making a living for "sick depend-

ents." I envy such women. I envy them as I never envied another human creature. They tell me, with simpers, how they "envy" me, and "how much you have accomplished, famous and all, while I am just a housewife," and I hate their complacent guts. Not one of them would exchange her life for mine, "fame" or not. They were brought up to be tenderly dependent—and they reap the rewards now of that upbringing. They lie in their teeth—and I don't blame them, really—when they tell me wistfully that they wish they'd had a career, too.

I told my daughters: "Marry men who will not permit you to work after marriage. Marry strong men who will take care of you and cherish you, and not tell you their business, and will refuse your 'help.' I had told them from the very beginning that unless a woman is powerfully (and by birth) motivated to the arts and the sciences and the professions, and is deeply gifted and cannot be denied, she should refrain from going out into the market places with mediocre abilities. Once she has earned a paycheck, I told my daughters, she is practically doomed—unless she can persuade a man that that paycheck is only a stop-gap before marriage, and she is only too happily willing to throw it over. She must then keep to her resolution: Never again to earn money outside her house. Never again to be a "partner, shoulder to shoulder with her man." Never again to be independent. In short, she should play the Big Con Game with her husband as shrewd and intelligent women have done for centuries.

I have accomplished the one success of my life: I have brought up daughters who have manly and cherishing husbands, who have never wanted to earn money outside their pleasant homes, who have concentrated on the sole and natural business of women: To be good wives and prudent mothers, soothers of the masculine brow, good cooks, pleasant companions, and truly feminine. I wish I'd had a mother just like me.

I fear that men are beginning to suspect that we women

conned them through the centuries. I fear they are asking themselves—to women's terrible hurt—why they should support an able-bodied woman who can earn a good living, too, and why should they be responsible for providing a home for women. Why can't women be architects and bricklayers and plumbers and stonemasons and lawyers and doctors and business women, too, and pile up a fat bank account to be inherited by husbands? Why should a man give his ex-wife alimony and child-support checks, when she is just as capable, if not more so, of rolling up her sleeves and getting on the 8:30 bus of a morning for an arduous day in the factory or the office?

After all, men whisper among themselves, women in Russia are treated *exactly* as men, and are farm-laborers plowing and seeding and harvesting, and they manhandle big machines in factories, empty garbage and shovel snow, learn to be bricklayers and steelworkers as well as doctors and lawyers, serve in the armies, drive trucks, wear felt pants, dig sewers and lay pipes, clean chimneys and work in the forests, and do the heaviest of manual labor.

The men listen to modern "Liberal" doctors who say— the cads—that women are much stronger and healthier than men, have more stamina, can do much more prolonged work, can bear children with ease and nonchalance, are healthy as horses, and therefore should do the heaviest of work and "take their places in the world, man to man." Too, women are now "sexually free," and so there is no need to marry them for amorous reasons. Most women, the men say, are eager and willing and aggressive, and ready for sport at all times, and are more zestful than men. So, who needs a wife, a bedmate, a woman to bear children? Let 'em work!

That's what men are already saying. They, too, have been listening to the Liberation Ladies, and the majority of them chuckle and slyly approve. The Liberation Ladies will lead to generations of women willing to support a tired husband, and provide for his old age. He can be snug-abed in the morning while she pounds off in her thick boots to her job, or carries a briefcase to her office. And when she comes home at night—she can cook his dinner, too, and wash and iron his shirts. She can do the housework, while he watches TV and complains of the pain in his back—which she will eventually rub away at bedtime. Women wanted careers, didn't they? They can do a man's work, can't they? Well, let 'em do it, and be glad they were able to get a husband besides, even if they have to take care of him!

Men, in short, are licking their lips and, for the first time in history, are readying themselves to be exploiters in their turn—to be the soft gentle creatures in the house, the soother of exhaustion, the serene person who has nothing to worry about in his pleasant life. Mom's out there, plugging and "fulfilling" herself, and why should Pop worry? He's had it coming to him since Eve.

Pick up any woman's magazine, particularly a certain one which was once run by men who promoted good articles and fiction and which was read by as many men as women. Read there the articles by shrewd sly gentlemen who proclaim a woman has as much "right" to a job or a career, as much "right" to be head of the household. Those boys know what they're up to: *The real enslavement of women.*

Tragically, such near-men and the Liberation Ladies can never crush the longing of a woman's heart, to be cherished, to be protected, to be guarded, to be honored, to be loved dearly and devotedly, to be a true helper, to be a complement, in her femininity, to the masculine nature; her longing to be the patroness of beauty and tranquility, to be the dear mother of respectful children, to be, as the Holy Bible says, "a good woman whose price is above rubies," the adorner of life, the civilizer, Godly, with beauty of spirit long after her youthful beauty has gone.

It is a woman's nature to make a sanctuary of love and delight in her home. That is the true "career" for women.

Alas, alas, that so many multitudes of women are now forced—or choose—to abandon that career, and to become imitation men in society. The true men won't marry them. The creeps will throng about them. They will reap the bitterness I have had to reap—though I never wanted a career, never wanted to be "stalwart." I just wanted to be a woman.

You really can't change human nature, and the instincts of that nature, for good or evil. I know a prosperous young man in New York, in his early thirties, who has a "pad" in a penthouse, and is up-to-date on everything, including Ladies Liberation. He highly approves of it. It is time, he told me, that women "stopped being parasites" and worked to the day they dropped dead or retired, as men do, and not expect a man "to support them." He is very enthusiastic, too, about women's "sexual liberation," and always managed to get a girl who, the dupe and dope, heartily agrees with him. "After all," says the young man, "women get as much fun out of it as men do, so why should a man feel obligated to them, or give them more than a drink and a dinner in exchange? I'm all for this new freedom for the girls."

He belongs to a Key Club. You know the kind I mean. When I was in New York recently he invited me to meet his "newest girl" at the Club. The "girl" happened to be a member of an advertising agency, a smart pretty cookie with swinging hair, and bright cheeks and eyes, and good manners, and an engaging way with her. Only her eyes were vulnerable, and soft and tender as she gazed at my young masculine friend. The lovelight shone in those eyes, deep and passionate and devoted. I thought these two hit it off wonderfully well, and I thought, too, what a wonderful marriage they would make and what handsome and intelligent children they would have. After all, the girl came of a good family, had a Master's degree in publication and advertising, and money of her own. And I could plainly see that marriage was fixed in her own ardent wishes and hopes.

When she went to the "powder room" I said to my sophisticated, progressive, and with-it young pal: "Are you going to marry Sally soon?"

He looked absolutely shocked! Suddenly the primitive man was there and not a "modern" man in a dinner jacket and black tie, in a Key Club with bunnies running around and the smell of winey cooking in the air. He was aghast. He said, "Excuse me, but you can't be serious, can you? Sally's all right. But, after all, she is a modern girl—she likes a romp as well as I do. No inhibitions." He paused. Then he said, "Playmates for play-time. *But only maidens for marriage!*" And he laughed.

When I still stared at him cynically he got a little mad. "Let's face it," he said. "The liberated girls have made their own public bed and they can lie in it, and we men love it. But if they think we are going to marry them they're due for an awakening. No man wants a woman who's been out on the town with every Tom, Dick, and Harry. When we marry we don't want a 'modern' woman." He laughed again. "Oh, we encourage the women to be 'liberated!' It's cheap for us, and we get all the free sex we want before we settle down with a *decent* girl."

Sally came back, glowing at the boyfriend, her heart in her eyes. No one ever told Sally that she was being used, that her womanhood had been cheapened and degraded by her sister-women in the name of "liberation." Sure, Sally had her "identity," as they wickedly call it, and her "freedom," and she was being fulfilled all right, all right! She had her good job and her independence and her nice little apartment . . . and she was twenty-seven years old and she would soon be middle-aged, and all she could marry then (and even now) would be some "Liberal" creep eager to live on her salary and permit her to support him.

The young man now opposite her, with his urbane manner and excellent income and ambitions, would never marry Sally. He would marry some sweet untouched creature who would not "stand shoulder to shoulder with him in the battle for life," but who would make him a pleasant little wife of whose decency he would be proud, and who had never heard the phrase, "women's liberation." Well, I suppose, it serves Sally right and all her deluded and pathetic sisters who sprint off to work every morning and take care of themselves and are as "free as men." But deep in their deprived hearts they know how tragic they are.

Girls, the men are catching on—through your sister-women who have been "liberated"—that they have been victims for ages of the Big Con Game, and the first thing you know they will be demanding Civil Rights and Equality for themselves, too! It's up to you, in behalf of future generations, to lull them back and to again become superior. Who wants Equality with men? No woman in her right mind!

Remember this: The strongest sign of decay of a nation is the feminization of men and the masculinization of women. It is notable that in Communist nations women are exhorted, and compelled, to do what has traditionally been men's work. American women, some of them, feel triumphant that they have broken down the "barricades" between the work of the sexes. I hope they will still feel triumphant when some commissar forces a shovel or an axe into their soft hands and compels them to pound and cut forests and dig ditches. I hope they will be "happy" when a husband deserts them and they must support their children and themselves alone. (After all, if a woman must be "free" she shouldn't object to men being free too, should she?) I hope they will feel "fulfilled" when they are given no more courtesies due their sex, and no kindnesses, but are kicked aside on the subways and buses by men, and jostled out of the way by men on busy sidewalks and in elevators.

I hope that no man will extend mercy to them because of obvious pregnancies, but will rudely tell them that that is no excuse to shirk a day's heavy labor, and they should be like Russian women. I hope they will be proud when some court demands that they support "delicate" husbands for a lifetime, and pay alimony. I hope, when they look in their mirrors, that they will be pleased to see exhausted and embittered faces, and that they will be consoled by their paychecks.

The decay and the ruin of a nation always has lain in the hands of its women. So does its life and strength, its reverence for beauty, its mercy and kindness. And above all, its men.

12

T.L.C.—Keep Your Paws Off Me!

As I am an enthusiastic hypochondriac, I had, a few years ago, worn to the very bone the local physicians and their catalogs of diagnoses. So, armed with brand-new symptoms, I went to another city which has a famous clinic, and entered its hospital for tests. I wasn't ill; I was simply curious to know what I had *this* time and if my own diagnosis would pay off to the discomfiture of my home doctors who had declared I was remarkably healthy.

The bed in my hospital room was comfortable and I had several interesting books to read, and so I prepared myself for a happy night of quiet entertainment. At midnight, hot on the trail of the murderer in a murder mystery, I heard the room door open and a youngish nurse, all arch tip-toeing, head-tiltings and enormous white teeth, invaded my room. Oh, darling, why wasn't I asleep? Did I hurt? Could she get me anything? Was I comfy? I looked a little, little tired. . .

While this soft monologue went on, the nurse began to

shift my well-arranged pillows, to smooth the sheets, to flutter her hands over my hair, actually to pat my cheek. I suddenly felt slimy. I got rid of the creature with a few unladylike words, and irritably lit up another cigarette. At 3 A.M. I turned off the light and went to sleep. Then, coming from the dark depths I was confronted by a brilliant flashlight, and another creature was bent over me, grinning, smoothing, patting, and squealingly demanding to know if I was all right. I was so shaken that I brought up oaths I hadn't used for years and routed her. It took some time to get calm enough to fall asleep again.

Before I was fully awake once more—and it was early morning and blasted sunlight was pouring into the room—my consciousness was aware of my hair being lovingly stroked, and also my cheeks and shoulders. I sprang up in bed with a yell, and still another nurse was smiling at me with simpering affection. "Morning, morning!" she trilled. "Time for our breakfast!" Apparently she caught some emotion in my face for she stopped suddenly, and fled. Wrathfully I waited for the doctor.

When he arrived I told him of my experience, and asked to be informed of the mental condition of the night-invaders. He was surprised. "Why," he said, taken aback, "there's nothing wrong with the girls! That's our new Tender Loving Care philosophy; it's supposed to lift the depressing atmosphere of a hospital."

I left an hour later. I now know why I had been suffering such belly-aches over a period of time and such intense irritability. I had been subject to Tender Loving Care in practically every area of my life, with the exception of my family, of course. It had been going on, it seemed, for years. It was the real cause of my nausea and acidity.

Now I recalled that I could not shop without having the saleswomen coo at me, smooth my arm, pat my back, or throw an arm about my shoulders. This had all embarrassed and annoyed me. Nor was this confined to shops.

Waitresses and waiters had taken it up, hovering like parent birds over the tables, smiling, beaming, peeking archly into one's face, solicitous and twittering. Had I been the only one who had felt annoyance and embarrassment? No; I recalled tight expressions on gentlemen's faces and looks of discomfort in the ladies' eyes.

Not long ago, loaded with luggage, I was stupid enough to stumble and fall flat on my face in an airplane on the way to my seat. Did the passengers and the stewardesses considerately avert their faces to spare me mortification, and allow me to pick myself and the luggage up and slide inconspicuously into my seat? They did not. Instantly warm, warm hands thickened the air about me; arms yanked me to my feet; the stewardesses cooed sweetly at me, assuring me that I was perfectly all right, darling, sure you are. Sick with humiliation, and enraged with myself for bringing all this "warmth" and "love" upon my person, I pushed away the clouds of helpers and found my seat. Did they let me alone? Not at all. The stewardesses took turns all during the trip to pat me, to flare their handsome white teeth into my face, to assure me that I was alive and uninjured. But I could have killed them in my outrage. During a quiet and unattended period a gentleman across the aisle looked at me sardonically.

"How do you like all this Tender Loving Care?" he asked me. He informed me that he was a physician employed by the airline company. "They're teaching the girls all about being motherly to the passengers," he said. "Hard on the girls. But the public laps it up, like syrup."

Maybe the public does "lap it up, like syrup." But only that part of the public which has a mendicant soul, a prideless and dependent character, a craven solicitude for its physical body, a maudlin desire to be petted, like a dog, by all and sundry. And this, by the way, is true only of America. Other peoples have more self-respect and would respond to such vulgarity with adult anger.

My husband, who blissfully believed he was a swimmer,

was taking a dip on a British beach some years ago. Coming to shore, in about a foot of water, he tripped and fell on his knees. At once the well-bred people on the beach politely averted their faces and talked to each other animatedly, thus sparing Leander humiliation and embarrassment. But I saw the same thing happen on an American beach, to a lady who was a remarkable swimmer. Instantly, with cries like mother birds, men and women surged into the knee-deep water, "rescued" the red-faced lady, and carried her in their arms to "safety." She tried to appear grateful, but I saw her eyes and grinned. It was so evident that she was indulging thoughts of violent mayhem on her rescuers.

Do your friends come up to you for a pleasant word when you are dining out? Ours don't, not any longer. They fall upon you with exclamations of affection, putting their hands on your arms, clutching your shoulders, playfully butting your chin with their fists. They exude "warmth." They know in their hearts that they are hypocrites, but it is all the thing now—this Laying on of Hands.

All this is the result of the social-worker psychology in this country, full of the desire to "help." Even the magazines have taken it up. Women don't buy their special magazines to learn how to cook or to read some light story. They buy magazines because they "care." It is never made specific what you are to "care" about. "Caring" is enough, and "being warm." What vomitous phrases!

My fellow conservatives are afraid that Big Brother is loose in the land now. This is bad enough. But Big Mama (of both sexes and the neuters, too) is infinitely worse, infinitely more dangerous to the national character, infinitely more demoralizing. She invades our privacy and reduces our dignity. Big Brother carries a club. Big Mama carries a bottle of stupefying and poisoned syrup. Let's send her back, all three sexes of her, to Washington, with a kick in her rump.

13

Luv and the Law

While writing on my novel about Cicero, the great orator, patriot and lawyer of Rome, I decided I needed some forensic experience, and so visited several civil courts, there to watch spectators, jury, judges, lawyers, plaintiffs, and defendants—not to mention the feverish comings and goings of social workers and psychiatrists. After a few sessions in various cities I know that I might just as well have stayed at home and read still more volumes on Cicero. The courts I visited were little different than the old Roman courts during the terrible decline of Rome from a republic into that democracy which was on its swift way to despotism.

Among many cases which appalled me was that of a burly teenager who had gone out on the street one night and beaten and almost killed an elderly and inoffensive old man. The "child" was well over six feet tall, weighed close to two hundred pounds, and had enormous hams on him and the face of an ape. The victim was frail and small, and his face was covered with healing scars and he trembled uncontrollably when he saw his assailant in court.

Little Billie, it came out during the proceedings, was "only" sixteen years old and an "unfortunate" school drop-out. He also came from a "broken home," i.e., his old man had "taken it on the lam" after a prolonged session with the bottle. Mama worked as a waitress, and looked worn out and woefully thin and drab of face. But did Mama receive any understanding from that jury, judge, or those spectators because she had a worthless lump of flesh for a son who had never done an honest thing in his life and who, from his earliest childhood, had been uncontrollable? Did the victim of Little Billie's vicious assault receive pity and consideration?

No, indeed. The sobs and sympathy were all for little Billie. Social workers spoke of his "lack of self-esteem," the result of having a mother who insisted on working outside the home, and a father who had an inordinate love for the stuff that did more than console. Little Billie, it was obvious from his size, had never lacked for groceries, milk, or vitamins, and his clothing was quite good even if off-beat in the usual manner of the young. One witness, a teacher, testified that Little Billie had always been incorrigible. With obvious disdain, the judge demanded, "Just what do you mean by that?" She testified that not only had Little Billie never manifested any respect for authority but that he had created constant disturbances in the schoolrooms, that he had once attacked another teacher, that he generally victimized children younger than himself, that he stole, lied, and never studied, and that he appeared generally unwilling to learn anything whatsoever. In short, though she did not say it, Billie was a slob.

The audience in this little courtroom drama was not with the teacher. She had disturbed their picture of a suffering infant who had been "underprivileged and disadvantaged" from birth. The teacher, who looked as worn as the mother of the slob, nevertheless showed considerable and admirable spirit, and was obviously no fool. Under an acid stream of mocking questions from the court, the public defenders, and the social workers, she did not quail or blush or retire. Did she know Little Billie came from a broken home? Yes, but so did many other kids! Did she know that Little Billie's Mama insisted on working outside the home when so many welfare agencies were "eager" to assist her with public funds? "Yes," said the teacher, wryly, "but she has some pride and sense of decency in a generally decadent society. My own mother was a teacher and a widow and had to leave five of us children at home, and we behaved ourselves."

Little Billie's still-trembling victim had been the recipient of unfriendly and murderous glances. Now the intrepid little teacher came into her share. One of the social workers accused her. "You don't understand children! You have no heart!" Restoring some measure of order, the judge asked the teacher if she had any suggestions about Little Billie's rehabilitation. Yes, she answered bluntly. A good, sound, severe reformatory where he would be taught to respect law and order and life. The courtroom growled into an uproar, and the judge scowled at her.

Little Billie was now led out of court, whimpering, hand in hand with a social worker half his size; and in disgrace, the teacher, the mother, and the forgotten victim walked slowly out together, huddling close to each other as if for protection. I stopped at the door, and said to the teacher, "What will become of that huge monster now?"

"He'll be pampered and petted, scolded sweetly a little, and then let loose on society to be an endless burden, or, most likely, he'll murder someone one of these days and thereafter be tenderly treated by a psychiatrist," she replied with some concern. "I don't know what's wrong with America these days! I see this sort of thing all the time."

In another court I encountered a far worse situation. A man of thirty was being held for molesting a five-year-old girl. He was married and a father himself. The child, brought into court to identify the criminal, screamed at the sight of him and had to be removed. But the molester sat in his chair and sobbed, and slowly those about him began to sob, too. I knew the routine by now. A psychiatrist testified that the molester had never had a chance. He had always been poor, never earning more than one hundred dollars a week in his life. He had never had what President Johnson declared "the basic necessities of life" —such as a new car, a television set, and household gadgets. His wife, he said, was unsympathetic. (She was under the incredible delusion that her husband ought to be a good father and show some manhood.) His parents had not "truly loved him" when he had been a child. Once he had wanted a pony and his father had cruelly declared that he could not have one. His mother had expected him to help out with household chores and the younger children. He had never been "permitted" to go to college.

At this point the angry lawyer for the parents of the abused little girl rose to ask a question. What in the hell, he seemed to be saying, had all this to do with the fact that the accused had molested a child? "Everything," the psychiatrist said firmly. One had to consider the "unfortunate" background of the accused; he was not less a victim than the little girl. The lawyer persisted. The accused had not been "permitted" to go to college. Why? Well, well. It seemed that he had been unable to do the work in high school because he had been "disturbed" as a child.

Would you believe it, the case was dismissed. The rapist was set loose, and he smiled smugly at the parents of his little victim as he was borne off in triumph by social workers. The slobs had won again.

14

Dolts and Love Cultists

The American insanity for Loving Everybody is ruining my good temper and delivering my stomach to enormous bouts with acidity.

I don't love everybody. There are in this Best of All Possible Worlds certain creatures who actually provoke my gentle and kindly nature to fits of genuine rage.

I was taught as a child to love and revere God, to love my country, to do my duty as a human soul in this world to which I had been committed. I was taught both spiritual and financial charity towards the feeble-minded, the permanently crippled, the hopelessly diseased, the blind, the halt, the aged who are unable to work, and orphans. But I was also taught not to be a malingerer, a weakling, a dependent on anybody—and I was taught to despise the Dolt.

On one occasion, recently, the House Committee on Un-American Activities met in the city where I live. It was immediately picketed by the students of the tax-supported university here, and some of their instructors. I took time off to study them. One and all, they presented a picture of spiritual and physical uncleanliness. It is possible that they occasionally wash and comb their straggling hair, but they did not give that impression. The days were cool and rainy, yet male and female wore sandals loosely tied over soiled bare feet; their clothing was drab and untidy; their faces were pallid and appeared strangers to to sun.

They came to frenzied life when they screamed at the investigating Congressmen. I am glad to report that there were few or no colored young people among them. I saw one, and he looked embarrassed. At last he drifted away, leaving only the "white folks" to parade and wail and denounce, and demand abolition of the harassed Committee. Of what are they afraid? That they may be compelled to be human, to be patriotic Americans, to be responsible men and women?

One of the deeply satisfying sights of that disgusting occasion was the appearance of some hardy construction workers—picketing the pickets! They had their own placards: "I am an American. Support the Committee!" I saw their strong hands, their firm and masculine walk, their rugged faces. By contrast, those picketing students, and their instructors, suddenly lost sex and became neuters, unkempt, and alien to work and to soap. They are the shame of America, the cultists of doltishness.

The Dolt believes that the world owes him a living, and particularly his more intelligent and industrious brothers. That is why he is always against the lowering of taxes. A cut in taxes might affect his precious dole from Washington or from local government; it might threaten the free lunches his children eat; he might have to *pay* to go to the zoo or art gallery or to a park. His kids might have to walk a few blocks to school instead of riding in tax-supported school buses. His favorite expression, uttered righteously, is "I gotta rightta—."

A few weeks ago a prominent politician wrote me frankly: "The Dolts hold the balance of power in the United States today. If I told them to go to work and stand on their own feet and behave themselves, and ask their neighbors for nothing, I'd never be elected again. I must yearn over them, assure them that they have the right to live at the expense of society, and that they have been 'abused by society,' and that they are 'underprivileged.' I must pretend to be a Liberal, slopping over with 'love' for them. It makes me feel dirty, sometimes . . . I am seriously considering not running for re-election next time. But if I don't, perhaps the Dolts will elect one of their own kind. They've already elected dozens in Washington as it is. I can at least help to stop some pending bills.

"Or, they have elected sinister men who are using them for their own purpose which, as you wrote me before, is their lust for power over a whole country. These Senators and Congressmen know exactly what the Dolt is, and they cater to him for his vote. But often they mutter in the cloakroom: 'Comes the day.' That day, I infer, is the day of a Soviet America."

If we are to survive as a nation we must shake the Dolt from our flesh, and cleanse ourselves of doltishness. It is time to rid ourselves of mendacious "love." It is time that we become angry. Angry at pusillanimous ideas and people, angry at liars and the degraded politician, angry at the panderers to the feeble, the hysterical, the traitors, the exploiters of our sentimentality. It is time that we truly loved—loved the manly and the brave, the steadfast and the true, the free and the proud, the patriotic and the just. Lest we choke to death on saccharine.

Many of the younger folk in their thirties are under the misapprehension that this nauseating love-cult began around the time Roosevelt was first afflicting the country. No. It began around the turn of the century.

I've never forgotten my first encounters with "love" on

a wholesale basis, without discrimination, without dignity, without respect for privacy, without decency. And each time I've come up against its massive stickiness, its outrageous impertinence, I've been freshly sickened. It has spread through every area of American life, an insipid and creeping huge aspic, blurring the edges of heroism and responsibility, setting awash weak millions in a sea of drifting sweetness, melting away standards and principles and virtue.

Worst of all, the most disastrous people in America have taken it up, and the curious thing about this is that the love-cultists do not extend their yearning passion to God, to the suffering millions in Russian slave-labor camps, to murdered Hungary, to Tibet, to the tormented satellites of the Soviet Empire. A hungry Spanish child does not move their love-bubbling hearts, but a Castro brings a beam to their eyes. The misery of the East Germans does not inspire them with manly indignation, but they write furious letters to Washington about the inhumanity of the white man in South Africa.

They have invaded our public schools with their love-cult, and so our young men and women in their teens continue to regard themselves as children long after puberty, and demand constant love from everyone with whom they come into contact. They have written so many books about a "child's need to be loved" that parents are afraid to slam their little monsters' behinds when caught in some particularly ugly offense. They have so cowed many of our clergy that the poor men no longer dare talk about sin, but only of "victims of society" and "lovelessness in the home," and Freud, of course. Children are no longer commanded to honor their parents; they are taught that *they* should be the honored. A policeman, formerly the guardian and friend of children, and a stern admonisher of potential little criminals, must not open his mouth unless he is a "pal" and "understands." The victim of a murderer is despised; the murderer is cosseted.

Love is too precious a thing to be wasted indiscriminately on those who eagerly take advantage of it and hold out their hands for more.

Only recently, a friend of mine, a fine man of high principle and devotion to his country, was defeated in a political election by a mediocre, mealy-mouthed man. Why? My friend was childless, and he had resolutely halted a scheme for spending enormous sums of money for unnecessary school-palaces with hot and cold running pools and with a proposed curriculum of homemaking, home economics, bird calling, folk dancing, folk stories, and social adjustment. But the mealy-mouthed man had five children, and he rousingly spoke of "spending more and more time with the kids," and could we afford NOT to have those lovely schools and the lovely program? Naturally, he won hands down. And why not? The love-cultists were right behind him, ringing doorbells in his behalf, getting up petitions, stealthily threatening the hard-headed and sensible, and accusing those who opposed them of "hating children." The matter of prudence, principle, patriotism, sensible administration, honor and righteousness and a regard for the hard-pressed taxpayer, was not even mentioned.

"Hate the Communists, if you want to," they tell you, "but love the Russians." The Russians want us to love them. We don't. And so they are bewildered, confused, angry, indignant, and perhaps just a little resentful. Who can blame them?

Yes, a professor said that to me only recently. When I refuted his maudlin and sinister premises, he did not look at me with love. He called me a "reactionary."

Sometimes I find myself choking on the insistent sweetness others try and force upon me. But one thing is sure; they don't love me, thank God! I have that to remember—that I've resisted successfully the attempts to love me and I have kept my right "not to be loved."

That is liberty. I refuse the right to be loved indiscriminately, without any effort on my part. I have only the right to earn it.

15

Plastic People

A few months ago my husband and I "dined" with a psychiatrist and his wife, both ebullient, bubbling and radiant.

Now, though I work anywhere from fourteen to eighteen hours a day, at the hardest kind of work, I eat but one real meal a day. I was always a fussy eater with a built-in dislike for food: no doubt due to the fact that my parents were British and were always downing five full meals a day, three of them heavy in meat. That's quite enough to make a sensitive person have an aversion to food for the rest of her life.

Besides, there's too much work to do in the world and too much to see and do to waste time filling your gizzard. Except when you are honestly hungry, after hard work.

The psychiatrist's wife first served a suspect-looking brown broth, which she delightedly informed the guests was "mock turtle." Later came something that bore a faint resemblance to lamb chops. But these had the most dreadful taste . . . "mock lamb chops!" We all smiled politely. Then, of course, there was a dish of "instant potatoes," a huge rabbity salad, some hot rolls that tasted of hay, a sweetish dessert covered with something white and whipped, and then tiny little cups of "health" coffee: that is, a brew minus all coffee and suggestive of something I will not mention. Now this was my meal of the day and I was hungry—and I ate. However, I still felt faint and depleted. I was soon informed why.

"Only four hundred and fifty calories in everybody's dinner!" our hostess said looking about her for applause. (She didn't get any.) Rather upset by our lack of appreciation and enthusiasm, she rushed out her recipes. Every foul thing on her menu was composed of near-synthetics or outright synthetics. For instance, as she proudly told us, the white, sweet-tasting stuff on the alleged dessert had not been cream at all. It was, and I quote the actual ingredients: "Polysorbate 60, sorbitan, monostearate, sodium citrate carrageenin, artificial color, water, vegetable fat, sugar." The "mock lamb chops" had been chopped, leftover cooked vegetables, flavored with "carameldin," and fried in "unsaturated fats." The potatoes had been cold, dried chips until they had been introduced to water, and the coffee—well, never mind. The only thing for real was that rabbity salad; and, as raw vegetables disagree with me, it made me sick within a few minutes.

"We all eat too much," the psychiatrist's lady confided to us as we groaned and quietly chewed dyspepsia tablets. "Don't you think so?" She looked earnestly at us; we had not said a word. She herself was in the large forties in dress size. I'll bet my next year's income that she privately intoxicated herself on real butter, real meat, real vegetables, and real cream and coffee. She had the look of those who actually become drunk on food, a fat and surfeited and greedy look.

And before we went home, we were introduced to her fake wool rugs, her fake silk draperies, her fake wood paneling, her fake carved furniture, her fake china ornaments, and so help me, her fake children.

How is it possible to have "fake" children? Mrs. Psychiatrist had managed it. The children were huge, pallid, empty-faced, stolid of demeanor, and had as much life as stuffed animals—which they resembled. They did not speak; they grunted or squealed, or both together. Their lifeless eyes had no living light. Their hair was nylon, by the looks of it. They walked jerkily, like automatons. They both had "dates" and went grunting and squealing out of the house, no doubt to some dark and airless lair, far from sunlight and moonlight and starlight, far from the great and swelling fragrance of the earth, far from grass and country roads and the winds of the solitary midnight.

Now one can understand the poor buying synthetic fabrics to imitate those of authentic sources. One can even understand "drip-dries" if one is traveling in a hurry or cannot afford laundry services. One might also understand the poor eating fake foods, like those of Mrs. Psychiatrist, if they cannot afford to buy the actual thing. But to buy synthetics in cold blood, with malice aforethought, and with more-or-less real money, is something I cannot understand. Worse, it's a deception, a fraud, and a lie.

Look at the chickens now on the market. Immense, flabby, insipid, tasteless. They have been pumped full of hormones to make a regular one-pound frying chicken a balloon-like monstrosity of three or even four pounds. There have been some mild hints from medical authorities to the effect that "one does not know if those hormones may be carcinogens." What "one" does not know about the food he eats will not later haunt him!

The market is now full of "taste-boosters" such as heavily salted and preserved chicken-fat, or beef-fat, or chemicals. We use the "boosters" or we resign ourselves to absolutely odorless and tasteless meals. Once, when a chicken was roasting in the oven a house was filled with fragrance. Once, when bread was being baked, or even bought bread was being toasted, the kitchen was lilting with heavenly scents. But now everything is deodorized —fake.

I remember that my mother brought silk-velvet draperies from England in 1907. When she died, in 1953, she had two pairs left, almost intact. But they were real. They were not "miracle" fabrics which fall apart in a couple of years, after a large initial cost. If these "new" fabrics were cheap one could avoid them, but they appear in the most lavish stores. Try to find honest-to-God cotton dresses, linens, curtains or whatever these days, or actual silk, or good hearty wool. Every infernal thing is "mixed" for "better wear," they say.

I remember when my husband managed, after some effort, to buy an all-wool suit. The majority were "mixed." Again, if they were cheap it would not matter so much. But one thinks of the average working-man, with his hard-earned money, buying fake goods of all kinds which will disintegrate within a short time. That is theft on the most cynical scale. One thinks, too, of the children growing up and trying to survive on suspect food, full of nasty, intruded chemicals and fluorides and "artificial flavorings." Are they never again to know cotton, silk, wool, linen, and the good taste of natural fowl and meat and authentic bread? Are they never to touch honest wood again, and stone? To what sort of a false and deceptive world have we introduced them, where everything fakes the actual, and nothing is sound and true any longer?

Can we expect such children to honor the noble actualities of patriotism, faith, honor, morality, loyalty, when they are surrounded by lies in their food and their drink, in their houses and in their schools? Can we expect the boys to be manly if there is nothing strong and masculine around them, and girls to be womanly if they are urged only to be "feminine"?

And that brings me to the heart of the matter. Once girl-children were taught by their mothers to know and cherish the arts of creating a home and the joys of devotion to children. They were taught to sew, wash, iron, cook, clean. They were taught modesty and piety, tenderness and chasity. In short, they were taught to be women. But what are they taught now? They are taught, by commercials and advertisements, and by foolish, childish mothers, to be cheaply seductive rather than naturally charming, to take a passionate interest in every passing fad and fashion rather than to love the abiding.

Little girls are early encased in false-front bras, and girdles. They paint their faces and bake their hair. They talk like tarts instead of young ladies. When they do speak of future husbands, they do not suggest that they'd prefer a man of courage and strength, fidelity and patience, intelligence and kindness. They squeal that they want someone who resembles the current singing "star" with "lots and lots of money for fun-times and clothes and furs." Of course, they confide to you, if the marriage they intend "doesn't work out" they'll get a divorce.

Once upon a time fathers taught their sons to be men, to be proud and fearless, brave and devoted. They taught them to love the Lord their God, and to go to church. They were taught to honor and to reverence their country; they were taught that only rascals are not patriotic; only traitors do not lift their eyes joyously to our flag. The "idle rich" were despised, not out of envy but out of honest disgust for worthlessness. The quick buck was regarded as contemptible. Mendicancy was intolerable and shameful. I have heard working-class fathers say to their boys, "Never eat the bread of charity. It will choke your soul." To acquire something one had not earned, and something which had belonged to a neighbor, was out-and-out theft to honorable Americans of yesterday.

But what are many of our boys today? Prissy, whining, cynical synthetics, almost sexless in their plastic sameness.

There is little to praise in them, no authority, no masculinity. They are kept from an authentic knowledge of life by their plaster parents; they are housed in playpens until they have been graduated from college. They are taught they are "children" when they are old enough to be parents, themselves. They are "youths" to middle-age. They are surrounded by inanimate or animated synthetics in human form. They bring their synthetic dream-world into adult relationships. Their wives must remain "young and attractive" into weary middle-age. Their wives must be "enthusiastic," no matter how hard the struggle during the day with little children. In short, their wives must be dream-images in a fake world, a world of neon mirages.

16

Why Not a SPUVV?

While all these proliferating societies are being formed, why not one called SPUVV, the Society for the Protection of Us Victims of "Victims"?

From the very dawn of history there have been "victims" of one damned thing or another, and all of them tearful and whimpering and dependent, and all of them, without fail, coming to us real victims for help and bread and gold and the blood of our sons and grandsons. If they haven't been "victims" of human tyrants, they have been "victims" of obscure diseases—all of them costly. No one begrudges helping a real victim, say of Communism or of the excesses of our own government, but why should the average American be forced to "aid" and "love" the Disadvantaged, Culturally Deprived, and Underprivileged, who are that way by the grace of laziness, sloth, their own addiction to mendicancy, and their passionate aversion to work? There isn't a day that my mail isn't flooded with appeals to aid the "victims," but it is a rare day when someone appeals for help in a fight against oppressive bureaucrats, sentimental judges, and vindictive social workers who want landlords to be "forced" to grace modest houses or apartments with luxurious "built-in" kitchens and gardens for the "deprived," or an extra bathroom to be used as a wood-storage receptacle.

Sympathy is poured on the "victims" by the tubful by all the brotherly-lovers who despise us mere toilers in the vineyards. Who pities the authentic victims? No bloody person, that's who.

I was three years old—ah, dreadful day!—when I was first a victim of a "victim." My gay Irish grandmother, when visiting us in Manchester from her houses either in Killarney, Dublin, London, Paris, Rome, Leeds, Glasgow, or Edinburgh, used to bring me a special delight which I think all the French call marrons glacés (sugared roasted chestnuts, first dipped in honey). They usually came in lovely tin boxes with a nymph on the cover in Full Color TV, without the peacock. Sometimes they came in milk-glass blown into the shape of a swan—very special, usually one pound extra in price. (Mama appropriated these, and that was one of the victimizations.) Anyway, on my third birthday Grandmother brought me my lovely delight in a beautiful French box, this time porcelain in the shape of a cello. I remember it well. I can't see a cello even now without a tear in my eye.

It seems that the boy across the street, a giant about five years old, had suddenly become Deprived. I'm not certain of what he had been Deprived, but he had. So, when Grandmother presented me with the china cello, perfect to the simulated strings, Mama said, "Janet, you have so many gifts, wouldn't you like to give Poor Kenneth that beautiful present?"

Janet said no at once.

Grandmother said, "Ann, why should the bairne?" Mama became very emotional. I clung to the cello, savoring the delights therein in anticipation. Mama said, "But the Poor Boy really needs the sweets more than she does."

Janet and Grandmother said simultaneously, "Who said so?"

Mama didn't dare slam Grandmother, for Grandmother had the Cash in the family, but I could see that she dearly wished to slam me.

"Is the lad starving?" asked Grandmother. "If so, take him some bread and jam and a bit of beef."

But Kenneth wasn't starving. At least I gathered that, for Mama looked scornful. It was something else, and what it was I never quite understood. Mama suddenly made a dive for my treasure, whipped it out of my hands, and as she was an old lady of twenty-one years she was forced to totter painfully out of the house with what she had incontinently swiped from me for the benefit of the "victim." I ran to the window, tore apart the curtains, and roared wildly when I saw Mama lay my gift, with flourishes, in the hands of Kenneth. Grandmother shook her head. "There's nae end to fools, lassie," she said. "Mind ye dinna become one of them."

The next day Unfortunate, Deprived Kenneth threw the china cello against our door and it was smashed to pieces. I looked at the wreckage with heartbreak, but Mama said with violin notes in her voice, "Poor Boy." (I noticed that none of the sweets were in the fragments, however.) At that age, three, I was, I confess, less Christian than I later became, so I went out and selected a nice pointed boulder from our garden, waylaid Kenneth that afternoon and cracked him over the head with it. It gave me almost as much satisfaction as eating the marrons glacés, myself, but not quite. My thoughts were very sinful.

It comes to me at this moment that the Unfortunate across the seas, or wherever, are constantly returning Uncle Sam's gifts with the equivalent of the smashed china cello——with the sweets eaten. Whenever one of our Embassies is stoned or burned or vandalized in one of the

Deprived Nations, I think of my darling cello, and I also think of pointed boulders.

Apparently other events of a similar nature happened to me in my childhood, though kind nature has softened the memory of most of them. I well remember when I was thirteen, and Wilson's War broke out. Mama and Papa, Britons both—and we were all in America then—became very stirred up indeed. I don't know how they, and my Sunday school teacher, wangled it, but I found myself, in the company of my best friend, Irma Jones, soliciting for Aid to the Allies.

Irma Jones was a colored girl. We were both big girls, standing heads over our mates, and unusually healthy and sturdy, and perhaps that is why we were chosen as victims. We took counsel together. Irma was a sensible young person, and she said to me, "Why're they fighting, anyway?" I said it had something to do with the Kaiser. He was cutting off Belgians' ears, it was alleged, though the Kaiser was also alleging that the Belgians were cutting off Germans' ears. It seemed less heinous to our parents and teachers for Belgians to do what the Germans were doing, though why I never did discover. They both bled and the process was undoubtedly painful. My arguments made Irma dubious, and she rubbed her own ears. "Well, anyway," she declared with the resignation of the victimized, and we set out on our collections, somberly plowing away on our skates. We had our doubts, but at least what we were doing was Approved, and as it was rare for us to do anything of that nature we were Uplifted —a little.

Our first victim was old Mr. Hurtz, head of the Hurtz Business School in Buffalo. Mr. Hurtz had a big crop of white hair, a knowledgeable eye, and a kind smile. I hit him for a contribution For the Allies. He pulled his immense white mustache and studied me. "Why?" he asked.

"It's Christian," I replied. Mr. Hurtz informed me he

was not a Christian. He smiled. "I guess it's a good idea," I said.

"Why?" he repeated. "They're always fighting over there, anyway. I was born in Russia, and so I know. You'd better keep out of it, sweeties."

Marvelous advice. Mr. Hurtz was far more intelligent than the Boys in Washington, though I did not know it at the time. He shook his head at me. He said to Irma, "Do you know what that war is all about?"

"No sir," she answered.

"Nobody else does," said Mr. Hurtz, "though everybody pretends to. All right girls, here's a dollar. I just hope it doesn't do any harm."

I'm sure it did.

Irma and I collected thirty dollars, a fortune in those days, and I don't know how we managed it. We did have thoughts of taking a small commission, say twenty percent, but Irma finally decided against it. "We must Sacrifice," said Irma, which just goes to show she was a born victim.

It was shortly after that when my pastor decided that the ladies of the parish—which included girls like Irma and me—should roll bandages for the Allies. As Irma and I had a good thing in the neighborhood, doing heavy chores other children wouldn't do, and getting paid decently for it, we balked. We had no time, we said. The pastor gazed at us reproachfully. "Don't you want to do your share?" he asked. We did not. We just wanted to be left alone, and work. "Selfish. Un-Christian," said the pastor. Irma and I, being very young then, had visions of hellfire. Irma had no history of marrons glacés in her past, as I did, she confided to me privately. "The boys are bleeding Over There," she said. "At least we can roll some bandages for them."

Remembering old Mr. Hurtz's wise remark, I said, "Why should they bleed, or fight?"

"Well, anyway," said Irma.

You will see she had a bad influence over me, for somehow I found myself rolling bandages alongside her. I never quite forgave Irma for that. Irma could roll like mad; I was more languid, resenting the nickels and the dimes I was losing every hour. Then Irma's mother taught her to knit, and inevitably Irma was knitting sweaters, but I could never learn to knit, thank God. By this time the First World War was a tremendous bore to me and I was not in the least uplifted by drums, banners, and bugles. Wilson was orating, but I never read his speeches. I began my first anti-war novel, which, however, was not published for nearly twenty-five years. Mr. Hurtz's bland cynicism had had its immortal effect on me. I read sections of my manuscript to Irma, who listened intelligently, but she always sighed and said, "Well, anyway. I guess nobody will ever know what it's all really about." Nobody ever did; and she was quite correct.

When I was sixteen I was working twelve hours a day, most of the time; six days a week, most of the time. I had exactly two dresses to my name, and one pair of shoes—the war wasn't over yet and Papa's firm was still not getting decent dyes from American manufacturers, and things were Tough. Came Christmas, and the boss suggested to me, and the male and female workers in his factory, that we each contribute something for Our Worthy Poor. (He was very well-off, himself.) I told him that I knew all about the Poor. They neither plowed nor did they spin. The whole damn country was getting worked up, at that time, over Our Unfortunate, who were comparatively prosperous, a number buying cars, something which my own father did not have.

The boss looked at me formidably and said, "Do you have any idea, Miss Caldwell, a well-fed woman like you, what it means to go hungry?"

"Usually," I said. It was always a toss-up with me for either lunch, fifteen cents, or carfare home, a matter of some eight miles, and even in the snow, too.

"I think," said the boss, with a dangerous look, "that you'd better give me a quarter, at least."

I had, alas, eaten lunch that day at a little shop down the street, and had no money at all. Payday was three days off. Then my slow Irish anger burned, and again I remembered my shattered cello and the loss of my sweets. "I'm the Worthy Poor myself," I said. "I don't have a cent, and you won't be deducting anything from my pay, either, or I'll call the police."

Of course, I lost my job immediately, but I found a better one three hours later. Irma's influence over me was practically over. But not quite.

Twelve years later the Roaring Stockmarket crashed, and all the world-be millionaires with it. Among the "victims" who had lost even their unmentionables in the Crash were two ladies in their thirties who had been operating a very lucrative lunchroom and delicatessen. On paydays I was sometimes extravagant enough to buy a quarter of a pound of ham from them and sometimes even some doughnuts, but that did not happen often. They each had a splendid car, fine clothing, took holidays in Florida—a place I could only dream of, enviously—and were Highly Invested, they told me with happy smiles, in the Stockmarket. "Fifty thousand dollars—me!" one would sing to those less affluent. "And I started with only five hundred! Just piled up!" They put nearly all their profits onto the paper ones they already had. "We'll be millionaires, soon!" they caroled. "We'll retire to Paris. Maybe. Paris in the spring!"

But the Market crashed, and suddenly there was a worldwide Depression, and the delicatessen ladies were penniless, the mortgage on their shop and apartment was due, their customers were no longer coming in and spending five dollars at a time, and the register had stopped tinkling. The shop closed. Four years went by. My husband had five dependents and had just had a fifteen percent cut in salary—courtesy of Roosevelt. Again, things were

Tough. I started to think of leaving my two young children alone and getting a job to help out. (Of course, we had never been able to afford a car or a holiday.) Then one dismal winter morning the doorbell rang and a very prosperous looking lady was on my doorstep, clad warmly in a nice fur coat. She beamed at me, adjusted her hat, and informed me she was "collecting."

"For what?" I asked. Her face seemed vaguely familiar.

"To tell you the truth," she said, "for my sister and me. We lost everything in the Crash. We're on Relief." She sighed. "We can hardly get by, and we get only fifty dollars a week from the city, and we can't get along on it. Victims of the Depression, you know."

Fifty dollars a week. That was just about what my husband was netting then, and there were five of us living on it—and not on Relief, either.

The woman was staring at me. "Say, don't I know you?" she asked. "Aren't you Mrs. Caldwell's daughter—don't remember your married name."

I recognized her then. She was the "Paris in the spring" lady. "You got it good, here," she said with envy, and held out her hand, palm up, demanding. Did I shut the door in her face, as any sensible young woman would have done, remembering? No, indeed. My silly heart burned with pity for her, and I gave her the dollar I had been hoarding. She stared at it with disdain, turned and walked down the stairs. I looked through the window. She drove away briskly in her car. With my dollar.

I remember this, when I pay my taxes for the War on Poverty, Operation Headstart, the Peace Corps, and all the rest of the Great Society—and for the Underprivileged and Underdeveloped Emerging Nations, and foreign aid for the Communists and Socialists who "never had it so good" as they do now—at your expense, and mine. Then, of course, there have been all those damnable wars to pay for, and probably more to come, to keep "the workers prosperous" and to "expand our dynamic economy."

We real victims are now allegedly fighting a war to "stop Communist aggression" in Asia. But in the meantime our tax dollars go to help support England's Welfare State, and England is doing a very sharp business, indeed, with our "foes" in Cuba and Vietnam, and so is Russia, the recipient of billions of our hard-earned money, and all our other dear enemies. We are victimized in our work, through taxes, and through the blood of our sons and grandsons, and we who have had three wars in one generation to remember are sick to death of it all in our hearts and our souls.

We have been victimized for tens of millions of "victims" all over the world, who are sassy and fat now and hate our guts. Washington is threatening us with a tax increase to "cool inflation," and we who are middle-aged, or old, are still desperately working to get a little ahead. But we'll find ourselves stripped of our substance—again —and our grandsons will be fighting more wars.

A few weeks ago, a grieving thirty-nine-year-old grandmother said to me, and her fifty-year-old mother, "My Roger is fighting in Vietnam, and we don't know what it's all about. What did you do, Mother, and you, Miss Caldwell, to stop all this in your own generations?"

We did all we could, we told her, and it was no use at all. Governments are too powerful for the individual, and governments are ruled by men who promise the worthless everything and threaten the hard-working with more confiscations of their fruits. That's how politicians get elected. We are as much victims as she is, we informed her. We worked and we studied and we struggled and we prayed —and we were treated with contempt by government for being such slobs. We ought, we said, to have sat down on our rumps, like millions of others, and insisted that our fellow Americans support us. In that way we'd have brought the country to crisis long ago—and that might have been a good thing. It would have shaken the lice out of the woodwork a couple of generations ago, and perhaps have cleaned Washington once and for all of the "brotherly lovers" who have now brought us to disaster. We are guilty, yes. We worked, and permitted our "government" to rob us.

Somewhere, we let the "victims" victimize us. Our government—God save the mark!—insists on "aiding" every lazy and "backward" or "underdeveloped" nation in the world. We must "spread democracy," even if other peoples neither want nor understand "democracy." As Mark Twain said, "Must we go on conferring our civilization upon the peoples who 'sit in darkness' or shall we give those poor things a rest?"

How about giving the decent American people a rest, too, from taxes and wars and the Poor, and the creeps and the Underprivileged, Culturally Deprived and Disadvantaged, and telling the whole damn bunch of those "victims" to spit on their hands and go to work—or starve?

Every once in a while—not often enough, alas—the victims get their bellies full of "victims." Then something happens, something that need not have taken place had the victims not permitted, for too long, their governments to victimize them. "Beware of the anger of a patient man," the old aphorism warns. Could it possibly be, please God, that us victims have finally become angered?

17

On Hippies

To understand the lawlessness, hatred for society, criminal tendencies, and revolt against authority, and the violence and hysteria of the hippie/yippies, it is necessary to study the causes, and the causes go back to their grandparents and their parents of over thirty years ago—long before this generation was born. I have studied those grandparents and those parents during their joyfully riotous heyday of the years of Roosevelt's War, and I, and millions of other concerned people, were very troubled and apprehensive then. We voiced our concern and were laughed down. We knew America was sowing the wind and would reap the whirlwind in this generation.

A prominent sociologist I know informed me recently that the offspring of conservative, law-abiding and decent parents—and grandparents—of the middle class often "revolted" and disagreed with their families, not to the extent of hippiedom, but in dissatisfaction and grumbling. This was quite normal and even healthy, said the sociologist, for youth always thinks it is superior to its forebears. Later, in their early twenties, the younger generation faces reality and settles down and becomes solid citizens.

But the hippie is entirely different. His grandparents and parents and himself were always, from the very beginning, in total accord with each other, and, in fact, the grandparents and parents are the main inciters today of lawlessness in their offspring!

There is no quarrel among them, just as there is no quarrel between the hippie and so many of the "liberal" faculties of colleges.

So, let us go back thirty or more years, when the grandparents of these riotous youths were themselves young and their to-be parents in elementary or the first years of high school. The Great Depression had been on for a decade, and the main sufferers had been the semi-skilled or unskilled workers, the majority of them decent poor people. But there was an element among them that was cunning, greedy, envious, incipiently lawless and usually not very intelligent and not very interested in bettering themselves. These latter had never adjusted to society, had never been industrious, had never been ambitious. But—while we were ostensibly still "neutral," they found themselves in war factories in America, and for the first time in their unproductive and careless lives they were receiving what they called "our big checks."

There was also a large element in the middle-class, too, of the same kind of mind and the same envy and resentment of people with better intellects and more ambition. They had, through inferiority of intelligence and drive, held only mediocre positions in the professions and in business. Rather than blaming themselves and their genetic inheritance, however, they blamed "society," whatever that is. They, too, when Roosevelt managed to get us into the war, found their under-average abilities in demand as "administrators" in various government offices and even in business offices. To their joy they also received "big checks" for their slovenly work, but their envy and rage against "society" did not abate.

They gave their distorted and sullen view of life to their children in elementary and high schools, and those children are now the parents of the hippie/yippies. For, you see, while virtue and good conduct are hard to learn and never too well regarded, lawlessness and hatred and rage are eagerly absorbed by the young. This is a fact of human nature which no realist can deny. Judeo-Christianity calls it "original sin."

The parents of the hippies—then in school—suddenly found themselves affluent through their war-working parents. They had never known luxuries before; they were not acquainted with moderation; they had never been disciplined. They roamed the streets shouting happily after school, their pockets filled with money. The characters of their own parents were too weak to impose authority on the young. So the parents of the hippies rampaged in movie theaters and on street corners and in schools, utterly out of control, though they did little of the violence their own children today are doing. They ranged through the shops in every city, buying heedlessly and extravagantly. Their own parents filled the saloons, roared the streets in new automobiles, crowded the restaurants and the shows, and were filled with euphoria. While young men died in Europe in the war and in the Pacific.

These were the people who were horrified and frightened when the war ended in Europe in 1945. But Washington reassured them that it would be "years" before Japan surrendered. Both Buffalo's newspapers carried that dispatch from Washington in their headlined accounts of Germany's defeat in May 1945. So, the war-working grandparents of these hippies of today were placated. The war would go on indefinitely, young American soldiers would continue to die, and the "big checks" would be constantly forthcoming. No one carried placards pleading for peace and withdrawal. There were no riots on the campus, no protests, no "marches." The war would go on.

Then the war ended in August 1945 with Japan's surrender, and immediately the grandparents of the hippie/yippies were more frightened and more dismayed than before. War production was cut down, though Washington, in August 1945, tried to reassure the "workers" that "there will continue to be bushfire wars to keep the war factories in production." I have retained the clippings. Now, at that time, "Old Joe Stalin" was in great favor with our government. "I like Old Joe," said President Truman, and this sentiment was happily echoed in Washington.

Now, with whom were the "brushfire wars" to be engaged in? No one said. It was enough for the public, that war production would continue, and the "big checks."

During this time the decent and sober sector of the citizenry was alarmed at the antics of the school-attending parents-to-be of the present generation of hippies. But all our protests were met with shrieks from parents and teachers: "Our wonderful boys and girls! There is nothing wrong with them!" Lawless they were, self-indulgent they were, greedy and careless they were, grasping and envious they were, and rather stupid they were, and incipiently violent. But—they were "our wonderful boys and girls."

Most of them became "dropouts" from school, because they had neither the will nor the intelligence to continue. Their parents were being told that "prosperity was here to stay," and they looked forward to decades of comfort, easy money, luxuries they had never earned, and perpetual "fun."

Many of us urged that they take up trades, seeing they could not really do academic work, which was then of high quality, or taught to earn a sober living. But again their parents and teachers screamed that these "wonderful boys and girls" should be "educated," and in consequence the curricula of schools and colleges steadily went down to meet their inferior minds and abilities.

A host of Communist-oriented "child psychologists" rose to declare that "environment" not heredity was "everything," and that any young person could be college-educated, if teachers "cared" enough to "help" them. Teachers tried. God knows, they tried. I know many of them and I know how desperately they tried. It was useless. And the curriculum of every school went down and down, and the good teachers quit in despair, or miserably shrugged and waited for their pensions. They told me so.

Progressive education had been tried in Russia, where it was believed that "environment is all." But the Russian Communists are hard-nosed and realistic. They found this was not so. So they discarded progressive education, and those in schools who could not meet the grades established were promptly removed from the schoolrooms and taught good sound trades and farming—at the age of twelve. However, America continued to support progressive education and is still supporting it today in most of our schools. It produced our hippies/yippies.

In the meantime, the "big checks" began to disappear, and the war production fell, and the grandparents of our hippies were outraged. It was all "society's fault." They taught their children envy and resentment, and hatred for the established law and order and authority. For, in their dull minds, they were convinced that their era of extravagance and easy money was not ended because of the end of the war but because "they,"—a mysterious "they"—were beginning to "oppress" them "again."

Their grandchildren, our hippie/yippies, call "they" the establishment, and they are in revolt against it. They want education without sweat and diligence; they want comforts without working for them; they want luxuries without any effort. They know their inferior minds will never serve them well, that they can never be truly educated, no matter how low the curriculum falls. They know they are misfits in the schoolroom. They know this subconsciously. But objectively they blame the "establishment." They want society to be dragged down to their level of accomplishment and intelligence. If society will not agree—then "society" as we know it must be abolished. They have animal cunning, but no intellect.

To digress a moment: I attended elementary and high schools in Buffalo. In the fifth grade we began to study ancient history, English literature and Shakespeare, Socrates and Homer, a foreign language and Algebra. We were expected, all of us in the fifth grade, to be able to write a decent and coherent essay on some advanced subject, and to be truly literate. By the eighth grade we had passed our Regents Tests in math, English, American and European history, civics and literature.

Now my teacher friends tell me with despair that these subjects—but not all of them—are taught only in the junior and senior years of high school, and then watered down. The other subjects are not even approached in college until the sophomore year! No wonder then that teachers in high school and colleges write me from all over the country that "this generation can barely read and write."

They, most of them, can't even write a simple declarative sentence! They are stupid and dull. The bright students are pushed aside in order to cater to the inferior and "advance" them. Intellect is suspect. The dull students are restive in class and disorderly and insolent and abusive. They can hardly be blamed. They are bored to death with subject matter they can never master. So, they think it is the fault of education, and that they, themselves, should choose what subjects they should learn! Worst of all, a prof recently wrote me from another city, that the young people don't blame their parents for their heredity. They blame their inability to learn on "the system." So, they fight all authority with frustrated rage and hatred.

They are aided and abetted by profs of their own background and of what used to be called "constitutional mental inferiority."

Twenty-five years ago "child psychologists" and "experts" entered the scene, with their fantasy-books on child-rearing. They denounced all discipline and all parental authority. A child was born "a blank page on which anything can be written," a foolish falsehood which any study of genetics can refute. A child must not be disciplined; it would give him a trauma. He must be pampered, protected and indulged. His adolescence must be extended even to the "late teens"! He was a "child" until he was about thirty. He must be protected from the bitter and dangerous reality of all existence. He must never be taught the truth. It might upset him.

He must be reared in a never-never land of "love" and softness and solicitude. He must be assured that the world was a "loving" place and not a natural arena of competition. Coddled and shielded, he came to believe that the world was just like mom's kitchen, warm and cozy and filled with the fragrance of baking chocolate-chip cookies, with a refrigerator full of orange juice and coke and endless bottles of milk. Everybody in the whole world loved him, he was taught by mom and his teachers and the child psychologists. He believed it. It was a happy thing to believe.

He never suspected that the world would "love" him only if he deserved love and worked for it, and that the world of men would judge him by his character and his industry and accomplishments. And that the world would reject him if he were slovenly, careless, insolent and uncontrolled.

When he discovered the truth he was not shook up from the false dreamland in which he had been reared. He was outraged. Something was wrong. It was not he and his parents. It was the "establishment." The "establishment" refused to "love" him for his indolence and his baby charm and the fact that he was "young," though by this time he was a full man in his late teens and early twenties.

Many of his grandparents and parents, when faced with

the fact that the era of big, unearned checks was over, became convinced, in some muddled way, that socialism and communism would restore the delight and euphoria of the war years to them. And they taught their children socialistic communism in their homes. In this they were encouraged, and taught, by the internal enemies of America:

The "liberal" profs and teachers and "leaders," and left-wing organizations, and child psychologists, and other misfits who could never adjust to the world of reality and so hated it.

Just recently I asked a pair of hippies, male and female —at least I think they were, but you can't tell these days—if they would be rioting, protesting, marching for "peace," and "dissenting," if we were fighting Hitler now. They both shouted, "No, we'd be the first to enlist!" "So," I said, "you don't really want peace. You just don't want Communists to be killed." They glared at me and said sullenly, "Yeah. That's it."

Indeed it is.

Just recently, when I took a long tour of the Pacific area, government officials in various countries said to me, "Why is it that the United States has supported, financed and advanced communism all over the world for the last fifty years?" I knew that we had, but it was disconcerting to learn that other "free" nations were well aware of what we had done for several decades, especially since 1945, through foreign aid and the Marshall Plan. If our government has taxed its citizens endless billions of dollars to rebuild Communist Russia, to secure slave countries for Russia, to safeguard the advance of Russia throughout the world, then we must not blame the hippie/yippies too much for their own communism. After all, it came right out of Washington, itself! An official of the Ford Foundation said, in 1958, that it was his hope and the hope of his Foundation that we would draw so close to communism that " we will merge peaceably with Russia." So, the hippies are not to be condemned alone. They are only repeating what they were taught.

Good teachers were replaced by teachers who were well indoctrinated in communism. The vast media of public communications were invaded and then taken over by left-wingers. Treason, anarchy, revolution and subversion were artfully written in books, produced in plays and on radio and TV, and printed in national magazines. It is a wonder not that we have so many rioting hippies but that we have so many decent young folk industriously working at good trades or studying hard—when they are permitted to do so—in schools and colleges. How they escaped the national corruption is a miracle. But it is hard to understand why the good and law-abiding majority of American citizens did not protest, themselves, from this universal and insidious degradation which has gone on for so many decades unchallenged.

At any rate, the cunning hippie is a misfit; he has no place in universities; he really has no place in orderly and industrious and good society. He will never make an adequate citizen or become responsible or reasonable. He will never amount to anything. He knows this in his corrupted and inferior heart. Hence, his war on what he calls the "straight" society, the society of civilized and self-respecting men and women.

What shall we do with this drug-wild and lawless creature? The trade unions could never teach him a trade, for trades today are sophisticated and require a good measure of intelligence and integrity. The hippie just does not possess the wit and skill to become an accomplished bricklayer, steel-worker, plasterer, plumber, machinist or mechanic. He hasn't the interior character to become a good teacher. He would perish on a farm, for he was never taught to respect labor and the land. He can never master the professions; he has no logical mind. (Can you imagine a hippie surgeon or lawyer?) His only desperate career, then, is criminal—if permitted—treason and revolution against the society from which he is barred, by his training, from ever entering. Of course, Russia has a permanent way of handling hippies, but I fear we would think it "un-Christian." We are faced with a terrible dilemma.

One of the fallacies of hippiedom is that the working man is "oppressed." So the hippie pretends, vociferously, that he is on the side of the working man—who loathes and ridicules him. He cries delicate tears over the "worker." Yet, when construction workers in New York and in other cities attacked the hippies, the true nature of the hippie came out. One of them told me recently, "When we take over, we'll put the . . . working man in his place, once and for all!" His face was full of hatred. Citizens—take notice!

We can, of course, protect ourselves from the hippie/yippie. When he shows force, we should show superior force. We can compel state-supported colleges—which exist because of our tax money—to expel the hippie and his faculty-sympathizer. We can raise the level of the curriculum to the height it was twenty or more years ago, and so the hippie would be automatically excluded. We can throw out progressive education in our public schools and demand that teachers teach again, and not indoctrinate with socialism. School subjects, not "love" courses or "social sciences," should be returned to the schools.

Diplomas should be issued in elementary and high schools only after severe examinations. Very stiff board examinations at colleges would weed out the intellectually unfit. A boy or girl of superior intelligence found in elementary and high schools should be given full scholarship to college. It is a crime that many of the brightest and the most able are kept out of university educations because their parents cannot afford it financially, just as it is a crime for the children of inferior intellect to be sent to college just because their parents can afford it.

We cannot afford the loss to society of the intelligent, just as we cannot afford the hippie. As the hippie usually has no morals or principles or character or self-discipline, he is usually a drug-user. To protect ourselves, we should make drug use and "pushing" one of the greatest crimes, on a par with murder—and pass laws to deal with them—even to capital punishment.

We can support our police, and demand of our governments that they support the police also. We should offer a police-career to capable young men of which they can be proud, with rewards such as high public respect and good salaries and esteem and prestige. After all, a man who risks his life to protect the citizenry is a warrior in the highest sense of the word, and he should be rewarded adequately. A police career should be on a par with any of the professions, and only the most intelligent and patriotic recruited. (Today the average policeman has more character and more intelligence than the average university prof!)

Once the police were deeply respected in this country. But our Communist-oriented society has degraded these brave men and has permitted them to be insulted by criminals, including the hippies, and even denounced by artful, sly and sentimental judges.

We can grimly make certain that any man appointed to a judgeship or elected to it is a man of the strongest and most principled character, a man of law and justice and good judgment, a man of integrity and honor, a man of patriotism and pride. Our hippies would not survive a week, or even the majority of our most flagrant criminals, if the judges everywhere were gentlemen of character and principle and virtue and had respect for the law and their country, and understood that it is their function not to protect the criminal but the decent citizenry against the criminal.

The criminal forfeits any "rights" when he attacks orderly society and duly appointed authority, but a lot of judges feel the victim of the criminal has no "rights"! Once the hippie-rioter and criminal understand that severe justice and punishment will fall on them swiftly when they transgress, the majority of them would fade away and torment us no more.

We can inform our elected officials that we insist on orderly government and the protection of the people, and that any politician who becomes maudlin over the criminal/hippie, will lose his job come the next election. We can demand, before any election, to know just where the aspiring politician stands on patriotism, sobriety, order, law and justice—and take no mealy-mouthed answer as an intelligent reply.

We can restore the love of God to our children, and teach them His ways and His ordinances and laws. When I surveyed the hippies on the University of Buffalo campus recently, my first anger was suddenly dissolved into pity for them. They are the Godless, the abandoned, by parents and teachers and the clergy. Their youth made them even more piteous. For their parents and grandparents took away their holy heritage, in this age of materialism and affluence, and too many of the clergy have led them astray into secularism.

They made me think of Mary in the garden, after the crucifixion of Christ. She saw the empty tomb and wept, and when the unrecognized Risen spoke to her gently she said, in tears, "They have taken away my Lord, and I do not know where they have laid Him."

An intellectual gentleman of many famous attainments is the Dean of the University of Edinburgh—Malcolm Muggeridge—a former "liberal," himself. But over these past few years he has become more than disenchanted with radical youth. He said, recently, that "they are not revolting against anything. They are just degenerate, really."

But the hippie did not spring from the ground by himself. He did not create himself. He is the product of lying and evil teachings, of envious and stupid grandparents and parents, of the national decline in patriotism and national pride and honor, of corrupt politicians, of lenient, sentimental judges, of national immorality and the toleration of wickedness, of the decay of character in the older generations, of his parents' abandonment of God.

Perhaps he deserves our compassion. Perhaps we made him what he is: Drug-obsessed, sexually degraded and perverted, suicidal, despairing, revolting without knowing why he revolts or against what he revolts. Perhaps we have put too much pressure on his mediocre mind so that he is wild with frustration. We expected more intelligence than he possesses.

We, perhaps, have corrupted our children and our grandchildren by heedless affluence, by a lack of manliness, by giving the younger generation more money and liberty than their youth can handle, by indoctrinating them with sinister ideologies and false values, by permitting them, as young children, to indulge themselves in impudence to superiors and defiance of duly constituted authority, by lack of prudent, swift punishment when they transgressed, by coddling and pampering them when they were children and protecting them from a very dangerous world—which always was and always will be. We gave them no moral arms, no spiritual armor.

We have taken away their Lord, and they do not know where we have laid Him. Until they find Him, they and our world stand under threat.